THE KING'S HIGHWAY

Kenneth R. Guindon

THE KING'S HIGHWAY

El Camino Real:

God's Highway to Peace and Happiness

FOUND AGAIN AFTER DETOURS
ON JEHOVAH'S WITNESS
AND PROTESTANT PATHS

IGNATIUS PRESS   SAN FRANCISCO

Cover design by Riz Boncan Marsella

© 1996 Ignatius Press, San Francisco
ISBN 0–89870–581–9
Library of Congress catalogue number 95–79948
Printed in the United States of America ⊚

TO MY MOST CHERISHED TREASURES:

My wife, Monique
AND
OUR CHILDREN
Jean-Philippe, Mireille, and Daniel

Also to Father Marc
Benedictine Monastery of Notre-Dame de Belloc
AND TO THE
Dominican Community of the Lamb
WHERE WE ENJOYED REAL Christian fellowship

Contents

Introduction

Growing up in California, I often noticed signs pointing out that Highway 101 followed the ancient route called *El Camino Real*. When I lived in Perpignan, France, again I saw signs marking another *Camino Real*, which passes through the town of Perthus on the Spanish border. Long ago, the Spaniards named their important highways *El Camino Real*, the Royal Road. In the New World, one *Camino Real* began in Veracruz, Mexico, and went all the way north to Santa Fe. Another of these famous roads was the route that followed the coast of California. Starting in San Diego near today's Mexican border, it wound its way north all the way to Sonoma. This is the road the Franciscans followed when they established their missions.

Our heavenly Father, the King of the universe, has laid out a road that I believe should be recognized as the King's Highway, or *El Camino Real*. While the Spanish highways followed the easiest route, it should be noted that God's road does not. It not only is narrow and sometimes difficult to identify but also has certain obstacles that require perseverance to overcome. One needs a lot of help when traveling on God's road, but the destination is worth any pain or suffering one might encounter. In spite of difficulties, peace and happiness can be found en route.

The King himself assures us that he will accompany us and provide us with the necessary help along the way. If someone finds the going hard, it may be that he is not allowing the King to show him the way. This is often the case with travelers who fail to study the map or read the signposts. Others will choose a path they think will be much easier but in reality is not. Instead, it leads them through swamps, jungles, or deserts, where they risk death from thirst and hunger. Insisting they need only to rely upon themselves, they deny that they lack adequate food and water. They persist in their refusal of help, even when they are ingesting something foul or poisonous. This metaphor is something we experience every day of our lives. The prophet Isaiah cried out to his people:

> Ho, every one who thirsts, come to the waters; and he who has no money, come, buy and eat! Come, buy wine and milk without money and without price.
>
> Why do you spend your money for that which is not bread, and your labor for that which does not satisfy? Hearken diligently to me, and eat what is good, and delight yourselves in fatness. Incline your ear, and come to me; hear, that your soul may live; and I will make with you an everlasting covenant, my steadfast, sure love for David.[1]

This book is written in the hope that forty years of personal experience will help others identify and follow the King's Highway. It is, in a sense, a confession, recounting the mistakes made early in life, but it is also a testimony demonstrating the power of God's grace to overcome those mistakes and bring forth good from them.

My story describes my Catholic background, the ways I was proselytized by the Jehovah's Witnesses, the sixteen years I dutifully served them, the reasons I left the Witnesses for evangelical Protestantism, and the events that led me back to life and service in the Catholic Church. Yes, one can lose his way, but my story proves that even one who is lost can discover the road home, *El Camino Real*, the true pathway of love and service to God and neighbor.

---

[1] Is 55:1–3. All quotations from the Bible unless indicated otherwise are taken from the Holy Bible, Revised Standard Version, Catholic edition, 1965, 1966 (San Francisco: Ignatius Press).

PART ONE

A Cradle Catholic Becomes a Jehovah's Witness

There is a way which seems right to a man, but its end is the way to death.

—PROVERBS 14:12

CHAPTER I

Growing Up in California

Born in November 1939, I grew up during World War II and the economic boom that followed. This period can be described as an era of growing wealth and independence for most Americans. The economy grew rapidly as a result of the industrial effort required by the war. The population became more mobile; many more people than ever before were able to afford an automobile and a new home. And so they came streaming out of the North, South, East, and Midwest to California in search of a better life. Most of them ended up in the Los Angeles area and on the old *Camino Real* along the coast.

Unfortunately, there was a negative aspect to this massive migration: many people were torn away from the extended family and community life in the smaller towns or ethnic neighborhoods of their origins. Many enjoyed a new anonymity that allowed them to throw off obligations and restrictions. No one was going to criticize them for not attending church, for example. And no one would notice if they practiced a new morality and ignored "outmoded" religious taboos. They thought: "I'm not any worse off than my neighbor", or, "If I go to hell, I certainly won't be alone." Many Catholics thought, "I obey the Golden Rule, I pray (sometimes), I go to church for the really big feast days, that's enough."

My parents were among those who had come to California seeking the "good life". They were of French Canadian descent; my father was born in Quebec, and both of my

mother's parents were from there. Mom and Dad had both
received a Catholic education. They were married in Woon-
socket, Rhode Island, which had a large French-speaking
immigrant population. But, as was true with so many "cultural Catholics", they were not close to the Church; they
were clinging (just barely) to a tradition. They had me baptized, and, thinking they were doing their duty, they sent me
to Catholic grammar school. That was, perhaps, more than
some other nominally Catholic parents did for their children,
and I am very grateful to them for that.

The United States entered the war against Japan and Ger-
many, and my dad was drafted and sent overseas. When he
came back after the war, it became apparent that he had developed a serious drinking problem. This caused a lot of
stress in the family and finally led to a divorce. Not long after
the divorce, when I was about eleven years old, my father
died. Seeing my father lying in the open casket was extremely difficult for me. He looked so different, especially
because I had not seen him for a while.

Mom and I continued to be on our own for the next
couple of years. I loved my mother, but sometimes I was hard
to handle. Mom often said that talking to me was "like talking to a wall". During this time I received little supervision
because Mom had to work full time to support us. The beach
was *the* place to go during summer vacations, so I spent most
of my time there with my friends.

Instead of going to Mass one Sunday morning, I left
early for the beach with my buddies. A big storm off the
coast of Baja California was causing huge waves along our
beaches, and I was caught up by one of these gigantic
breakers and swept out far from the shore. I will never forget this terrifying experience. As the current was pulling
me farther and farther out, all I could think was, "I'm going to hell. I have committed a mortal sin because I didn't
go to Mass this morning!" It seemed incredible to me that

I, who had been an altar server for so long and had tried to be good, was going to hell for one single lapse of obedience.

I have no recollection of family prayers or discussions about God. My mother did have me say my prayers at night before I went to bed. That was the extent of it. The only advice on this topic that I do remember receiving was: "Kenny, there are two things you should never discuss with others: religion and politics. If you do, you will have arguments and lose friends."

When I was about eleven or twelve, Mom asked what I wanted to be when I grew up. She encouraged me (more than once) to consider becoming a doctor, a lawyer, or some other highly esteemed professional. I told her that I wanted to become a priest. In fact, I asked her if I could go to minor seminary. "You can't possibly realize the seriousness of what you're saying", she responded, explaining that some day I would want to marry and have children. "Besides," she added, "we don't have the money to pay for a seminary education." That ended the discussion.

Two years after my confirmation, I left the Church, as did many of my peers. I did not intend this to happen. I simply drifted away because no one took me to Mass regularly or encouraged me to go. My idea of religion and getting to heaven was that you simply had to be lucky enough to die at the right moment. The best timing would be soon after having made a good confession.

Mom eventually met someone she could love, and they married. I was happy to have a new dad. We celebrated my thirteenth birthday, and I received a new .22 caliber rifle, something I had been wanting for a long time, and we all went camping and fishing together. Family life had really taken a turn for the better! We even acquired an extended family through my stepfather's relatives. Only one thing was lacking, but I didn't notice it. We never went to church as a family. We never thought about it, and, certainly, we never discussed it.

Upon my completion of the ninth grade at Saint Monica's, a Catholic high school, Mom and Dad decided to send me to public high school. They explained that I could get a good education there, I wouldn't have to take the bus, and the family could avoid unnecessary expenses. Like any other boy my age, I didn't want to leave the school where I knew everybody. Nevertheless, I began my sophomore year at Santa Monica High School, a big change from a much smaller private school. The first couple of years were uneventful. The school was "tougher", morality was loose. These are exactly the years when morality needs help, but we had no help there. The most striking result of my move to a public school was that I no longer had *any* contact with the Catholic Church.

CHAPTER 2

Trapped in the Web of Discussion

> No lie is of the truth.
> —1 JOHN 2:21

Careful students have observed that many people enter a cult during a time of stress or uncertainty. Suffering from unemployment or stress due to problems like divorce, sickness, or the death of a loved one, they are searching for answers. In what appears to be an answer to prayer, someone knocks at their door or approaches them on the street. Here is a friend who is confident and optimistic and apparently has the solution to their problems. In my case I was no longer attending Mass, and I hadn't been to confession for a long time. I knew I needed to put my life in order, but, like many others my age, I figured I had time for that. At sixteen, I enjoyed going to the beach, bowling, horseback riding, and just hanging around with my friends, none of whom went to church either.

When my buddies and I planned a trip to Tijuana, Mexico, we stayed overnight at my friend Jay's house. We planned to get up early in the morning to make the trip. None of our parents would know where we were going. That night, as we spent time in Jay's living room, I overheard his mother, Ruth, talking to my friend Louis about the Bible. Louis was a Mexican American and a Catholic. I had already noticed Ruth's magazines, which attacked the Catholic Church's teachings about Mary. I asked Louis if he minded if I stepped into the conversation "to defend my Church". After all, hadn't I spent

seven years in Catholic schools? I thought I was better prepared than he to defend our faith. This is where I made my
first mistake; I stepped right into a trap. Let me describe how
the typical Jehovah's Witness, like a spider, spins a web around
his victim.

Does God have a name?

Ruth, a mature woman around forty-five years old, began
questioning me. "Well, Ken, what have you learned in your
Church? Do you really think the Catholic Church is telling
you the truth about God? Can you tell me what God's name
is?" "Well," I replied, "his name is God." "No," she said, "try
again." After a moment's thought I said, "Oh, I know what
you want, his name is Jesus!" "Wait a moment," Ruth re-
torted, "that can't be right because Jesus said we should pray,
'Hallowed be thy name.' He surely wasn't praying to himself,
was he? No, he was praying to his Father in heaven. You
know that Jesus is the name of the Son of God, so what is his
Father's name?" There I was stumped, humiliated. I just
couldn't seem to see what she was getting at. I had never
heard of anyone talking about God having a name. God was
God, and that was it. You called him Father at times, or Lord,
but did he have a name like us? These were questions she
forced me to consider. (This is what she wanted: an opportunity to put herself into the driver's seat, to become my
teacher.)

Using the Bible, she explained that there are many gods
and many lords, and this is why God has to have a name to
distinguish himself from all the false gods that are worshipped by the various peoples in the world.[1] She told me the
Bible clearly teaches that there is only one God who is the
Father above and only one Lord Jesus Christ who is God's
agent (1 Cor 8:6). As the Christ (Messiah) has a personal

---

[1] 1 Cor 8:5, "many 'gods' and many 'lords' ".

name, Jesus, so the Father also has a personal name that he wants us to sanctify, honor, and make known.

Would I like to know what his name is? Would I like to see it in the Bible? "Okay," I said, "show it to me." And so, opening her Bible (King James Version), she read to me from Psalm 83:18, "That men may know that thou, whose name alone is JEHOVAH, art the most high over all the earth." I couldn't remember ever hearing that name before. (Years later, when thumbing through my ninth-grade religion book, I saw that I had been taught the name Jehovah, but I had not taken note of it.) There it was—God has a name, yet I had been raised and educated as a Catholic and didn't know his name! It made me feel as if I had been betrayed.

The second point in which she got me enmeshed was a point of logic. She asked me if I believed the Catholic Church to be the one and only true Church. I told her that I firmly believed so. To this Ruth replied: "If such were the case, wouldn't it be *reasonable* to expect that whatever the Catholic Church teaches as truth would be in harmony with the Bible, since the Bible is God's inspired Word?" She supported that with Jesus' statement: "Thy word is truth" (Jn 17:17).

IS THE SON EQUAL WITH HIS FATHER?

Several days later, we again took up the discussion. I was a little excited, and we were jumping from one topic to another. I liked talking about God, and I sincerely wanted to know more about the Bible. I hadn't the slightest desire to become a Jehovah's Witness. I knew nothing about them, apart from something I had heard during grade school. I had been on the school bus and had asked my buddy who the people were standing on the corner, displaying some magazines. He told me he had heard they were communists, because they didn't support the government or salute the flag.

In my discussion with Ruth, moreover, I was happy to

imagine (oh, how innocent I was) that I was going to defend my religion. I was more than a little proud to expound what I knew. (I didn't realize that I didn't know anything substantial.) At first, I was simply having fun, enjoying a good debate. At the same time, I discovered I had learned a lot (even though I didn't accept any of it yet) in the few hours I had spent with Ruth. She was patient and really seemed to know the Bible.

Ruth continued pounding me without letup: Could I explain the Trinity to her, she wanted to know. Did I understand it? Is Jesus really God, the Second Person of the Trinity? I told her that this is what I believed; yet, I had to admit that it was a mystery. She argued that if the doctrine about the Trinity were true and so important, why couldn't we find some clear statement of it in the Bible. This sounded logical. Pressing home her point, she challenged me to prove the Trinity to her from the Scriptures. Of course I couldn't; why, I had never read anything in the Bible before meeting her. I didn't even know how to use it. You would have thought that having studied for seven years in Catholic schools and having been confirmed, I should have known something about the Bible. I had learned a number of definitions from a catechism, but I had never been trained to defend my faith.

Ruth confronted me with more apparent contradictions. She asked me if I believed Jesus to be equal to the Father in time, nature, and power. "Sure he is," I replied, "because he is God the Son." She challenged me to find such a statement in the Bible. Would I believe Jesus' own words on the matter as recorded in the Gospels? "Why not?", I said, although I was getting a little piqued at her smugness and her ability to find a verse for every little thing.

Turning to John 14:28, she read Jesus' own words to me: "The Father is greater than I." What could I say to that? How could Jesus be equal to his Father in heaven and yet say that his Father was greater than he? There must be an answer somewhere, I thought, but where? Surely a priest would know; I just lacked the training, the ability to explain it to her. The only thing I could think was that Jesus had two natures, a human nature and a divine nature; this had to be the answer. But then she asked me to explain how Jesus could die if he were the immortal God?

Ruth told me that her organization used a translation of the New Testament that was more accurate than other versions. It was called the *New World Translation of the Christian Greek Scriptures*.[2] She explained that its very title showed that it didn't follow the traditions of men. She wanted to show me that because Jesus was the Son, he couldn't be equal to his Father in time. Since he had received life from the Father, he could be like God, but he never could be God himself. Furthermore, this proved that he couldn't be eternal, because he had a beginning. Taking the JW[3] New Testament just mentioned, she read to me from John 1:1: "Originally the Word was, and the Word was with God, and the Word was a god." Next, she showed me two other Bibles, one translated by James Moffatt and the other by Edgar Goodspeed,[4] scholars who never were Jehovah's Witnesses. Both translations said the Word "*was divine*".[5] This was done to prove that the New World Translation wasn't unique or radical when it said "the Word was a god". All this was supposed to prove that, although he was like his Father, Jehovah, and could be called "a god", he was not God Almighty. That's pretty heady stuff for

[2] *New World Translation of the Christian Greek Scriptures*, 2d ed. (Brooklyn: Watchtower Bible and Tract Society [hereafter WTBTS], 1951). Various editions of the New World Translation will be quoted as: NWT.

[3] JW: an abbreviation for Jehovah's Witnesses that I will use throughout the book.

[4] Edgar J. Goodspeed, *The Complete Bible: An American Translation*, rev. ed. (Chicago: University of Chicago Press, 1939), and James Moffatt, *A New Translation of the Bible, Containing the Old and the New Testaments*, rev. ed. (New York: Harper & Row, 1954).

[5] Jn 1:1, emphasis added.

a sixteen-year-old Catholic lad. In reply to every one of my protestations, she would reply: "Okay, show me where the Bible says that." And then she would show me three or four Bible verses to support her beliefs.

WHAT IS THE END OF MAN?

I was now a frequent visitor in Jay's home. One day Ruth asked me where I expected to go when I died. I explained as best as I could that if I died in a state of grace I could hope to go to heaven. She wanted to know how that could be possible (of course, she knew what I would say). I explained that we have a soul and the soul goes to heaven or hell (or purgatory) at the moment of death, depending upon what kind of person one is at that particular moment. Of course she wanted to know if I were eager to die so that I could go to be with God in heaven. At age sixteen, I assured her, I thought I could stand to wait a while for the great event. I certainly wasn't in any hurry. She said that seemed to be the case with most so-called Christians. They are never in a hurry to die, but they hurry to call the doctor even when their problem is minor.

Like every well-trained JW, Ruth wanted to show me how it might be possible never to die. She wanted to convince me that God has a plan for mankind and for the earth, man's home, and all this was on the point of being realized. Here she began spinning a truly fascinating tale. She explained that we were living at a very special time in history and that Jesus Christ would return soon to put an end to man's suffering and to all wars. She told me how this Second Coming of Christ would usher in a new world of righteousness, peace, and prosperity for all those who accept the Witnesses' message (this is the JW gospel). She supported all her statements by quoting passages from the Bible.[6] A snare had

---

[6] For example: Gen 2:8; Ps 37:1, 9–11; Is 65:17; 2 Pet 3:13; and Rev 21:1–5.

just been placed at my feet. Would I be caught? My Church hadn't told me about this good news; could it be true?

After building her case about living forever upon the earth, Ruth returned to the subject of the soul. "What does your catechism say about the soul?" she asked. "Is it immortal?" I replied, "Yes, because it is created in the image of God, it is immortal. It survives the death of the body." She told me that, years ago, Charles T. Russell, the founder of the Jehovah's Witnesses, had often challenged various clergymen to show a single Bible verse that says: "The soul is immortal." With a sly grin, she said that she would offer five dollars to anyone who could find one passage that states the soul is immortal. Well, I suspected I would be out five dollars, because I couldn't tell Generations from Revolutions (Genesis from Revelation).

Again she asked me whether I was willing to accept God's Word on the matter. Pointing to Ezekiel 18:4,[7] she read: "Behold, all souls are mine . . . the soul that sinneth, it shall die" (KJV). She explained that someone is a soul. One doesn't *have* a soul, one *is* a soul. How could we be sure of this? Ruth said that one only had to turn to the history of man's creation in Genesis and he would see that this is clearly the case. With her guiding me, we turned to Genesis 2:7 (KJV) and read: "And the LORD God formed man of the dust of the ground, and breathed into his nostrils the breath of life, and man became a living soul."

---

[7] The Jehovah's Witnesses were in the process of translating the Old Testament, and so when quoting from it, Ruth used either the American Standard Version of the Bible, rev. 1881–1885, and newly edited by the American Revision Committee in 1901, standard edition (Camden, N.J.: Thomas Nelson Inc., 1901), or the King James Version. The American Standard Version is a revision of the King James Version (and an ancestor of the Revised Standard Version) and uses the divine name Jehovah where the KJV uses LORD in capital letters to represent the Hebrew tetragrammaton (four Hebrew letters for Yahveh or Yahweh). The Watchtower Society (agency of Jehovah's Witnesses) had printed the ASV since 1944.

Using the Oxford reference edition of the King James Version,[8] she showed me from the marginal readings the original Hebrew word. For example, one learns that where the KJV has *creature* (Gen 1:20, 21, 24) or *soul* (Gen 1:30), the original Hebrew word is *nephesh*. Why is this important? Ruth said: "If we search *Strong's Exhaustive Concordance*, which has a Hebrew and Greek lexicon in the back, we can see how the word *nephesh* is used throughout the Old Testament. One will discover that a soul has an appetite (Is 29:8), that it can be killed or destroyed with the sword (Jos 10:28, 30, 32, 39), and that the Messiah would pour out his soul unto death (Is 53:12)." She also showed me that *souls* (i.e., persons) who refuse to receive the Messiah and his teaching would be destroyed (Acts 3:23).

Another important point to learn, she affirmed, is that the Bible says the soul (i.e., *life*) is in the blood (Gen 9:4, 5). If one loses his blood, he loses his life or soul. Therefore, soul is limited to two possible definitions: a person, a *living creature* (this also includes animals that breathe [Num 31:28]), or the *life* a person or animal possesses (Gen 1:30). So if *soul* refers to the person and not to an immortal spirit we possess, we can easily understand why Ezekiel 18:4 says: "The soul that sins shall die." This is what happened to Adam because of disobedience (cf. Rom 6:23). Elsewhere, the Bible even speaks of dead souls (Num 6:6; 9:6, 7; 19:13).[9]

Like Adam, all disobedient persons will die, Ruth explained. The meek and teachable will be resurrected to life on earth, which will become their home for eternity (Ps 37:9; Mt 5:5). Men and animals will live peacefully together

---

[8] *The Holy Bible* (London: Oxford University Press, n.d); this edition, with notes and references in a center column, also points out alternate readings. This is the edition I have used for many years.

[9] References can be found under *soul* in *The Englishman's Hebrew and Chaldee Concordance of the Old Testament*, 5th ed. (Grand Rapids: Zondervan, 1970).

(Is 2:4; 11:6–9). This will be possible because men will have been fully tested before being considered worthy to receive eternal life. A thousand-year period is coming, in which the people of the past who never had the opportunity to learn about Jehovah's plan will be resurrected and given a chance to accept or reject it. If they accept it and pass the final test at the end of the millennial reign (Rev 20:1–3, 7–10), they will be deemed worthy to be adopted as God's sons and live forever (Rev 20:12).[10]

I must admit that such ideas were extremely fascinating to a sixteen-year-old. Everything seemed so logical, so easy to understand. Every point seemed to be anchored in the Scriptures; for there was Ruth with her Bibles, manuals, a concordance, and even an interlinear Greek-English New Testament (*The Emphatic Diaglott*),[11] to back up everything she said. She certainly could not have been faulted for a lack of training or effort.

Having discredited the idea of an immortal soul, with gun still smoking, Ruth turned to shoot down the doctrine of an everlasting hell. For the most part, she used passages from the Old Testament (as she had done with the topic of the soul) to prove that hell is merely the grave (e.g., Ps 146:4; Qo[12] 9:2, 4–

---

[10] Support for this can be found in the following book—even though it had not yet been published when I began studying with Jehovah's Witnesses: *Life Everlasting—In Freedom of the Sons of God* (Brooklyn: WTBTS, 1966), p. 400.

[11] Benjamin Wilson, *The Emphatic Diaglott* (Brooklyn: WTBTS, 1942). This was originally published in 1864 by B. Wilson, a newspaper editor. Mr. Wilson held many ideas similar to those taught later by the Watchtower Society. Therefore, the use of this book to authenticate JW doctrines was quite devious! "The plates for *The Emphatic Diaglott* came into the possession of the Society in 1902, although it was previously used by the Bible Students" (i.e., older name for Jehovah's Witnesses). See Edmond Charles Gruss, *Apostles of Denial: An Examination and Exposé of the History, Doctrines and Claims of the Jehovah's Witnesses* (Nutley, N.J.: Presbyterian and Reformed Publishing, 1970), p. 191, n. 2.

[12] Qoheleth, also called Ecclesiastes.

5, 10). Ruth told me that a person is unconscious in the grave and therefore cannot be subjected to pain or torments. Next she showed that the word *grave* comes from the Hebrew word *sheol*, which is translated *hell* in many of our older Bibles. This is where Christ went after his crucifixion (Acts 2:24, 27). With a friendly smile on her face, she asked: "If the soul doesn't survive the death of the body, how can there be a burning hell or place of torment for it? If God is love, how could he torture the ones he has made in an everlasting fire?" I shouldn't be afraid of hell but rejoice at learning that I now had a chance to live forever on a paradise earth, like the one in which Adam had been placed. I shouldn't let the Church terrorize me with threats of hell, she advised.

All along, Ruth had been trying to convince me that the Catholic Church had been lying about the Scriptures. More boldly now, she explained that the Church wanted only to make money by telling ignorant people they must have Masses said for the dead. The clergy was wicked, she said, and she accused them of teaching pagan doctrines that they had inherited from Babylon of old. She especially went after the popes and religious of the Middle Ages. She told stories about monks and nuns building tunnels between their monasteries so they could indulge in illicit relations. Then, to hide their misdeeds, they aborted the children they conceived and plastered the fetuses into the tunnel walls.[13]

All this was convincing and intriguing, and so I agreed to study a lesson a week with her. I had already learned so much from our discussions. But I was really hoping I would be able to prove that she was wrong. We used a little manual called *Let God Be True, Though Every Man Be Found a Liar.*[14] Ruth explained that it would help us keep on track and avoid

---

[13] I learned only recently that Maria Monk, who claimed to have been a nun, was responsible for such stories. See Catholic Answers' tract *Anti-Catholic Whoppers*.

[14] Rev. ed. (Brooklyn: WTBTS, 1952).

jumping from subject to subject. We spent many happy hours together. She showed me how to use the Bible and a concordance. Until then, no one had ever spent time talking about God with me personally.

In addition to teaching me about the Bible, Ruth also presented the JW version of Christian history, detailing the moral failures of both Catholics and Protestants. She sought to discredit everyone but the Jehovah's Witnesses. Pointing to the two world wars, she asked, "Would Christ and the apostles have accepted being drafted into the nations' armies? Finding themselves dispersed in different countries, would they have been willing to take up arms against each other?" Well, Ruth assured me, JWs weren't anything like these false Christians. They were united; they all taught the same thing; and, what's more, they truly loved one another. Ruth said they were exactly like the first Christians. That summed up everything she wanted to prove.

Jesus had said that his disciples would be like sheep in the midst of wolves, and wasn't that the case with the Witnesses? They were persecuted by all the other religions and the politicians. Hitler, "an ally of the Catholic Church", had persecuted them and put them in the concentration camps. All the communist countries banned them, too. She proudly pointed to the persecution they suffered in the United States. She related how people had tried to force them to salute the flag, going so far as to tar and feather some of them. She told how they had maintained their religious freedom only after long court battles, some of them even fought before the Supreme Court. All this persecution was inspired by Satan, who is the god of this world (2 Cor 4:4). The devil inspires the world governments and the religions to unite together to fight against Jehovah's Witnesses, against the *truth*, against the preaching work (Rev 17:1, 2).

As Ruth continued contrasting false Christians and worldly people with the Jehovah's Witnesses, she also en-

Kingdom Hall, in Venice, California: constructed in 1957 by
Ken Guindon and other Jehovah's Witnesses

couraged me to attend their meetings. Jay and I began attending and making friends with the young people there. We exchanged our "worldly" friends for new JW friends. I began withdrawing from family activities. I refused to go on camping trips and to celebrate birthdays or other holidays. I spent weekends helping to build a new Kingdom Hall, i.e., JW meeting place. When I was home, I argued with my parents and attacked other religious groups as evil.

As I got in deeper and deeper, my family life deteriorated. My stepfather forbade me to continue studying with Ruth. He said the Witnesses were a bunch of communists because they wouldn't salute the flag or fight for their country. He asked me what I would do if the "commies" attacked our home; would I defend my mother? The question hurt. My parents warned that I could be imprisoned for refusing compulsory military service. They quarreled with me, and they argued with each other. Each night, I could overhear my parents discussing me in their bedroom across the hallway from mine. My mother was fearful she could be faced with a bill of divorce if I continued causing so many problems in the family. I have no doubt my involvement with the Witnesses damaged my relationship with my stepfather. Finally, he clammed up, completely stopped talking to me. He would not even ask me to pass him the salt at the dinner table. I was sorry about it, because I had really liked and appreciated him. (Thank God we now have a good relationship once again.) But Ruth had foretold that I was going to be persecuted, so I felt I was being tested. Would I hold up, I wondered. Did I love Jehovah and Christ Jesus more than my family? This was the choice the Witnesses said I had to make.

In contrast to the lack of appreciation I received from my parents, the people at the Kingdom Hall were giving me loads of encouragement and showing their appreciation for the tough time I was having at home. They said I was a "tremendous fellow" for accepting the truth and taking my stand for Jehovah and his organization. They told me I was right to ignore my parents' warnings. After all, they were "opposers of God's kingdom". Jay, who also was having difficulty with his father (an atheist), became a very good friend.

Toward the end of my senior year, I was in turmoil. The tension at home was painful, to the point that I even broke down and cried a couple of times in class. Having studied with the Witnesses for almost a year, I was preoccupied with many questions: Is God a Trinity? Did Jesus found the Catholic Church? Is Armageddon coming soon? Would the JWs be the only survivors at the end of the world? I was reading and studying a lot because I wanted to know if the Witnesses possessed the truth. Wanting to see a priest, I went to the parish in which I had been baptized, Saint Monica's. How disappointed I was by the priest's way of reasoning. He did not simply open his Bible and demolish the Witnesses' arguments. In fact, he opened it only once. I had fully expected him to have the answers I so desperately needed. I truly wanted him to vindicate my Catholic beliefs. I did *not want* to become a Jehovah's Witness. The priest gave me philosophical reasons as answers to some of my questions. Unfortunately, I quickly lost patience with his approach. The Witnesses had already convinced me that everything must be proven by the Bible. I wanted proof from the Scriptures that the Catholic Church was, indeed, God's Church. Because I believed the priest had failed to answer my questions, I went against my parents' will and was baptized by immersion during a local convention of Jehovah's Witnesses in Hollywood. I was seventeen years old.

CHAPTER 3

Doctrines and Indoctrination

After graduating from high school (I refused to attend the ceremony because Witnesses are not allowed to stand for the national anthem), I spent all of my free time with the Jehovah's Witnesses. Every effort, every moment was focused on gaining eternal life.

According to *The Watchtower*, the official journal published by Jehovah's Witnesses, if one wants to receive eternal life he must, first, take in accurate knowledge of Jehovah God and Jesus Christ (Jn 17:3, NWT). For the moment, I will only mention that their translation of the Bible is very tendentious and oftentimes erroneous. Arguing from John 17:3: "This means everlasting life, their taking in knowledge of you", they tell us we must study with them. While attending Bible studies one learns next that he must become a member of the organization, be baptized by immersion, and then go from door to door to persuade others to begin this process. A member is obliged to attend five meetings a week and be an active preacher for JWs. This is the meaning of their name, *Witnesses*. It's a religion geared to peddling literature and convincing others to join their movement in order to escape Jehovah's impending wrath upon unbelievers.

The new convert is obliged to leave behind the world, i.e., pagan holiday celebrations, military service, labor unions, voting, and family and friends who are not JWs and so not "in the truth" (Jn 17:16, 17). No problem; he now has new friends, ones to whom he will become very closely attached. They are his new family, his *real* brothers and sisters. This is how they address themselves. "Why, hello, Brother Thomas, Brother Ken, and Sister Ruth. How are you?" The JW's religion involves a total commitment. In addition to the weekly meetings, members are expected to attend circuit, district, national, and international conventions, which often require a lot of travel and expense. I attended the international convention in New York City in 1958. There were a quarter of a million people in attendance from 123 countries and islands.

It may surprise you to learn that the Jehovah's Witnesses actually are a government within a government. They believe that they are ruled by Jehovah God through Jesus Christ and the 144,000. The Watchtower Bible and Tract Society, Inc., is a corporation they use legally to print literature and to represent Jehovah's Witnesses. (They have other corporations, and sometimes the name Watch Tower is used. This explains the differences in some footnotes.) So, first of all, they believe they are receiving instructions directly from heaven through a channel composed of the body members of Christ, i.e., the 144,000 (Rev 14:1–5). Since the 144,000 began to be called at Pentecost when the Church was born, there are very few left. They report that there are only about 8,600 on earth today. To be one of the directors and on the board of the "governing body", one must claim to be one of these specially anointed members of the 144,000. These together compose the Church, or spiritual Israel (Rev 7). Jehovah's Witnesses have their own laws; they hold trials to discipline and excommunicate members. They say their government is *theocratic*, i.e., ruled by God. Even the Bible belongs to the "organization".

> [T]he Bible is an organizational book and belongs to the Christian congregation as an organization, not to individuals, regardless of how sincerely they may believe that they can interpret the Bible. For this reason the Bible cannot be properly understood without Jehovah's visible organization in mind. . . . The Bible sets forth every inducement and en-

couragement to place the theocratic organization ahead of oneself, to accept it in all its features and stick to it loyally.[1]

The little group composing the governing body numbers twelve members today.[2] It is a self-perpetuating body. In my time with the Witnesses, this "governing body" did not exist as it does today. This is something they developed around 1972 to involve more people in the decision-making process. Before about 1972, the president of the Watchtower Society was the strong decision-maker, and the vice president, Mr. Fred Franz, was known as their "Bible scholar". The Society's officers, president, and vice president are elected in a rubber-stamp meeting held in Pennsylvania for shareholders who approve the names put forward by the governing body. There is never an electoral process where several candidates are put forward for the same office. The governing body is broken down into various committees, such as a personnel committee, a publications committee, a service committee, and so on. The *1993 Yearbook of Jehovah's Witnesses* gives a good presentation of the organization and the use of the expression "spiritual Israel".[3] It is important to note in my various quotations of Watchtower literature that all written material is approved in Brooklyn, New York; it is printed either there or in the various branch office factories around the world. In 1995, Jehovah's Witnesses claimed over five million members throughout the world.[4]

The leadership emphasized three issues: Jehovah's sovereignty; the vindication of his name, Jehovah; and our need to refuse to be a part of this world. After becoming a member of the "New World Society", an expression the Witnesses

---

[1] *The Watchtower*, October 1, 1967, pp. 587, 597.

[2] *1993 Yearbook of Jehovah's Witnesses*, Spanish ed. (Mexico: WTBTS of Pennsylvania, 1993), p. 253. The Spanish title is: *1993 Anuario de los Testigos de Jehová.*

[3] Ibid., pp. 253–55.

[4] *The Watchtower*, January 1, 1996, p. 15.

used during the fifties, we were to remain obedient to God's rule as manifested in the "Society". In practice this meant bondage to the Watchtower Society's views. No one is allowed to question the correctness of their interpretations (you were supposed to have done this before joining), because they believe they are a "spirit-guided" organization united in the pure worship of God. When JWs were few in number, they boasted that only one family had the truth and survived the flood of Noah's day. Since they now number in the millions and have become quite wealthy, they say this is proof of God's blessing.

Having become a fervent believer in Witness doctrines, I attended the Sunday lecture, followed by a study of *The Watchtower* magazine. Tuesday evenings I attended the "book study" (usually held in someone's home), and on Thursday evenings I went to the Theocratic Ministry School[5] held at the Kingdom Hall, and then, during a second hour, we attended another meeting called the "Service Meeting". Each meeting lasted one hour, and so we attended five hours of meetings a week. In the Ministry School, I was given simple seven-minute assignments that allowed me to become accustomed to speaking before a group. My knees trembled when I got up for the first time before a crowd. Suit and tie were required dress for the meetings and for witnessing from door to door. This door-to-door work is called field service and is considered a part of our worship, therefore it was not to be neglected. Anyone who didn't take part in the field service couldn't call himself one of Jehovah's Witnesses.

Every subscription to *The Watchtower* and *Awake!* magazines, all magazines and publications we sold, and our time spent in this activity were to be posted on a form we had to turn in at the Kingdom Hall. We were asked to do this once a week or, at the very least, once a month. This allowed for

---

[5] This school was organized in 1943 to train JWs in public speaking in the local congregations.

close supervision of each *publisher* (the name used for each JW worker). Each month, the congregation sent Brooklyn headquarters a report of the service totals and the number of active publishers.

The headquarters sent a *circuit servant* (later called *circuit overseer*) to visit each congregation. He visited and supervised a group of some twelve congregations. He checked on the work being accomplished by each congregation and sent a report of the results of his visit to Brooklyn. He spent time with the *servants* (now called *elders*). He investigated the growth, took note of weaknesses and local problems, and gave lectures to correct and motivate us. He visited the irregular and the inactive publishers to encourage them to serve Jehovah while there was still time.[6]

I was assigned a trainer to work with me and teach me the necessary techniques for the door-to-door work. Since I was now employed and working nights, I spent many an afternoon and Saturday and Sunday mornings working with him. He was a *pioneer*, meaning he spent an average of one hundred hours a month in the field service. He supported himself working as a bricklayer, since he was not paid for his witnessing work. JWs love to point out that they don't have any paid preachers or clergy; they are all volunteer workers for Jehovah. Of course, some do receive an allowance because they are giving all their time to the work and have a special appointment from the headquarters. These people include the headquarters staff, called the *Bethel family*, the special pioneers, the circuit and district servants, and the missionaries who are working in a foreign country.

My trainer took me along with him from door to door. Watching him, I learned how to give the short presentations that we memorized from the *Kingdom Ministry* sheets we re-

---

[6] An irregular publisher is one who misses turning in a field-service activity report for any month during a period of six months. An inactive publisher is one who no longer participates in the field service.

ceived at our Service Meetings. In those meetings, we practiced giving door-step sermons, learned how to present the
books and magazines, and memorized the Society's answers
to objections we met in our ministry. We had ready answers
to a variety of objections, such as: "I'm busy right now";
"I'm not interested"; "I have my own religion"; "I'm Jewish!"; "I'm Catholic!" or, "I don't believe in God." I watched
my trainer handle all these, never getting ruffled or put off.
He taught me how to get the magazines into the people's
hands, making it difficult for them to hand them back when
they didn't want them. We said: "These are your copies"
(putting them in their hands); once they were holding them
we added, "for a contribution of *only* ten cents." After each
presentation, he analyzed my approach and my style and he
gave me appropriate counsel. After a while I could give the
entire presentation myself and go to doors alone. He worked
on one side of the street, and I on the other; he was close by
if I needed him. He also taught me how to fill out my reports
and turn them in each week.

Nadine, his sister-in-law, became my girlfriend. At seventeen, I was in love. One might have called it infatuation, but
to me it was serious. We spent hours on the phone talking
about the coming new world, the paradise earth in which we
hoped to live. Yes, I wanted to marry Nadine and raise children in a paradise. Why would I want to live in this old world
with its sufferings, sickness, and death, with its hypocrisy,
wars, and false religions? No, nothing was any good here; all
that mattered was Jehovah's Witnesses, the new world, and
being faithful until death.

I believed my old Catholic and Protestant friends and my
parents were going to be destroyed at Armageddon (Rev
16:14, 16) if they continued opposing the truth. This is what
I told my mother the day I left home. I was so blinded, so
entrapped in a web of lies and promises, that I could think
only of the New World Society. I was no longer a part of this

world; I was totally involved in another world, one of doctrines, study, and preaching. I was told not even to think of furthering my education. One doesn't need a college education to preach the truth about God's name and kingdom, JWs said. University was discouraged because it exposed one to dangerous worldly knowledge, influences, and temptations. We needed to make the most of our lives by becoming pioneers during the "short time remaining". In 1941, *The Watchtower*, "God's channel of truth", went so far as to speak of the "remaining months before Armageddon".

PART TWO

Serving Jehovah

Ye are my witnesses, saith Jehovah, and I am God.

—ISAIAH 43:12 (ASV)

(from the cover of *The Watchtower*, 1950)

CHAPTER 4

Pioneering in Maine

A lot of young Witnesses were saying they were "AAA"—available after Armageddon. This meant that they were not planning on marriage until God's war destroyed all the wicked on earth (Jer 25:33). Because we believed that the end of the old world was near, we wanted to work hard in the field service, to make sacrifices in order to become pioneers, to forego higher education, and to postpone marriage and children. This last point had been strongly recommended in the past, especially in the publication *Children*.[1] This book gave, as an example for young people to follow, John and Eunice, who put off their marriage until after Armageddon. JWs thought it was better (more spiritual) to delay marriage and children until after Armageddon, when the earth would be cleansed of all wickedness. Now was the time for work! When I became a Witness, not having children was not stressed as much as in earlier years, but celibacy was and is considered a better way (1 Cor 7). Nevertheless, even the Watchtower Society's president, Nathan Knorr, had married. In fact, all of their presidents have been married men, except for Fred Franz.

In spite of my zeal for Jehovah, I was devastated when Nadine broke up with me. I was miserable during the meetings at the Kingdom Hall. I sat there watching her, dreaming of her, praying to be able to get back together with her. Would I ever be happy again?

---

[1] *Children* (Brooklyn, N.Y.: WTBTS, 1941).

A certain phrase had been brought to our attention at conventions and service meetings: "Serving where the need is great". The young people turned it around and said, "where the great are needed". Since I was unhappy in California, I thought, why not go serve Jehovah somewhere else, somewhere where the need is greater? Besides needing to get away, I really did want to serve God and give my life to him. It had been a lifelong dream. So I began to think of becoming a missionary. They didn't need *me* here in California; the proportion of Jehovah's Witnesses to the population in California was really very high. Other states or regions had very few Witnesses, so people in states like California were encouraged to move to these regions and become pioneers. Because I was a nature lover, I began thinking of going to Utah. I wrote the Watchtower headquarters in Brooklyn, explaining my desire to pioneer, and telling them of my readiness to move to Utah or any other state, even to Madagascar if they wanted. I wanted new surroundings and, most of all, to give my life more completely to God's service.

Motivated by this goal, I quit smoking (condemned by the Society in those days and later a reason for excommunication) and increased my hours. I told the congregation servant, who was also Nadine's father, that I wanted to go into pioneer work. Recognizing my need for more experience, he and the other elders began giving me more assignments in the Service Meeting. Finally, the Society's reply arrived, suggesting Maine as a place where the need was very great. The letter described a town in northern Maine called Houlton, where there were already a pioneer and a special pioneer[2] from Massachusetts. Some young people also were there helping them for an indefinite time. The headquarters gave some names of other locations to consider: Caribou, near the Canadian border, the Auburn-Lewiston area, and Bidde-

---

[2] Special pioneers had goals (requirements) of 150 hours a month and received an allowance of fifty dollars per month at that time.

ford in southern Maine. All these places had a large French-speaking population. It sounded very exciting, so I began making my plans to leave my beloved California.

After working a year, I had nine hundred dollars saved for my trip. When the Society announced an international convention in New York for August 1958, I planned to attend on my way to Maine. I would cross the country in my 1953 Ford. This would allow me to bring all my books and clothes. It was a step of faith for me. I was glad Jay agreed to accompany me as far as New York City. Finally, the end of July and the date to leave arrived.

Leaving behind L.A., we headed out across the Mojave Desert. After driving all day, we arrived in the early evening in Las Vegas. We decided to walk and stretch our legs a little in the streets, so we visited a casino and got invited by the bouncer to leave (we were under age). We just told him we had been kicked out of better places than his. We took off again, driving nonstop all the way through Utah and into Wyoming. We were exhausted. Driving at night was horrible. Since we couldn't take any more, we decided to spend the night in a town called Rawlins. Lying there in bed in the motel, I thought about how far I was from home. It suddenly hit me rather hard. I had left home. How were things going to turn out? How would I live? Would I find work? I have to admit that I was a little scared; but, I thought, Jehovah is with me and he will help me. So, the next day, we turned our faces eastward again and drove on to Nebraska, where we spent a couple of days on a wheat farm with relatives of Jay. We helped them harvest and store the grain. I haven't forgotten this first experience working under a scorching sun—the humidity, the sweat, and the dust.

Once we arrived in New York, we went to our assigned accommodations, which the preconvention workers had found for us. New York City is an impressive place for a couple of young men from Santa Monica. Seeing the crowds at the convention, we knew that Jehovah was blessing his people. Everywhere we went—streets, buses, and subways—Jehovah's Witnesses were to be seen. They were easy to spot. Some placed copies of *The Watchtower* in their car windows to identify themselves. When we saw them, we honked and waved and shouted, "Hey, look, there are some brothers and sisters." It was exciting. All of us proudly wore our convention badges to identify ourselves as Jehovah's people. Of course, it had another purpose. We were advertising. We were free walking publicity for our religion, so we had been advised to watch our conduct. Some JWs volunteered to wear placards; they were "sandwich" men or women and handed out invitations to people.

Our eight-day convention finally drew to a close and along with it an unforgettable time spent with Jehovah's people. More than 253,000 people came to hear the closing Sunday lecture. I said good-bye to Jay, my longtime friend, and got out the maps again. This time I had to travel alone. In one long haul I made it to southern Maine, where I stopped to visit the overseer of the Auburn congregation. I was looking for the place where I would start my career as a pioneer, a missionary for the truth. From there, I went north to Houlton. It was a small town but could boast of having a college. Aroostook County, Maine (at least at that time), was said to be the potato capital of the world. Eventually, I was going to learn more about potatoes than just picking them off a plate. Because the Houlton congregation was responsible for the biggest territory in Maine, and there was a group of young people working temporarily with the two older and more mature pioneers, I decided to stay in Houlton.

The service department at the Watchtower Society's headquarters in Brooklyn responded favorably to my application to enter into the pioneer ministry. I pledged to do my best to meet the monthly goals: spend one hundred hours in field service, distribute one hundred *Watchtower* and *Awake!* magazines, make return visits, and conduct at least five Bible studies. Meeting these goals was not easy. First of all, a Witness is dealing with people who usually have their own religion, which they think is right. This means that much of the witnessing work is rather aggressive, confrontational. The JW missionary is asking the other person to put his religion in question, to imagine that for many years he has been living in error. If he hasn't been kicked out at this point, the Witness will eventually go so far as to say that the priests and ministers of other denominations are insincere and deceiving the people. He wants an opportunity to prove to anyone who will listen that the churches' doctrines are false, wicked, and inspired by the devil. Eventually, he will let the person know that other churches are "whores" (Rev 17) who have prostituted themselves to the politicians (James 4:4).

So one can appreciate that a JW often is given a cool reception at best. In Maine, where it was known that some years before I got there a JW had killed a man, people just slammed the door in our faces. I even had people threaten to get their gun if I didn't immediately leave their property. Others used another strategy: they challenged us to pray with them and only then would they listen to us; others told us they would listen to us if we would agree to salute the flag. Of course, we couldn't do either of those things.

Another obstacle was the weather. The summers were beautiful, as were the autumns, when the woods were resplendent with bright colors. But winters in Maine were extremely cold and snowy for a Californian. I remember waking up one morning and finding that the sheets we had hung up indoors to dry had frozen solid. They could not be hung up outside because the snow had reached the height of the clothesline. Some mornings, when we left the house, the temperature was around five or ten degrees below zero. The snowbanks along the country roads were often over our heads.

Despite the weather, the pioneer has to maintain his

monthly goals. If he gets sick or snowed in, he has to put in more hours to make up for the lost time. If the car fails to start because of the cold, he has to walk to reach his territory. It's not hard to imagine how glad I was when some nice lady invited me inside and let me talk. I learned a little "trick" from the older and more experienced JW. When someone opened his door just a crack, we would stamp our feet on the doormat and say, "We don't want to keep you at the door, may we come in?" or "I don't want you to lose your heat with us standing here at the door; may we come in? We won't be long." This device did not work very often, but often enough for us to keep trying it.

On a few occasions when the weather was inclement, I stayed home and wrote lengthy letters to my mother. I told her all about my experiences and gave her as many points of doctrine as I dared. This, too, was considered witnessing, and the time spent writing to her could be counted toward my monthly goal. Another trick we pioneers employed on frigid days was to record the amount of time we spent in the car. We would drive a couple of blocks in the direction of the territory we wanted to canvass, pile out of the car, and each one of us knock on a door. Then we would quickly return to the car and drive twenty or thirty minutes more in the country and repeat the procedure. By now we had clocked an hour of field service while driving to the town where we were to work.

We "regular" pioneers were obliged to work part time to support ourselves. I was able to work in the fall potato harvest, which earned me enough cash to last a while. Forming a team with another person or with several others made it possible for us to meet expenses, but I remember times when we were really destitute. We would each put four dollars a week into the "kitty" for food, so we were really grateful when someone gave us some canned ham or something else they had received from the state welfare department.

The difficulties I faced during that first winter were experiences that molded my character for later life and the many challenges I would meet. They taught me to trust in God, to persevere, and, not least of all, not to fear men.

After I had been in Maine a while, I was appointed the Theocratic Ministry School servant in the Houlton congregation. We had only a handful of people, probably no more that fifteen persons of all ages. We were also responsible for fifteen or twenty interested people in Patten. At least once a month we would visit that group, hold meetings with them, and preach in their locality. I remember a lady's reply to my knock on the door in Patten. Trying to get rid of me, she aggressively told me that the previous Sunday her minister warned the congregation that Jehovah's Witnesses don't believe that Jesus is God. With my sweetest voice possible, I assured her that this wasn't true. I said, "Ma'am, we do believe in the *divinity* of Christ; in John 1:1, the Apostle John says that Jesus is divine. [I was, of course, quoting the translations by Goodspeed and Moffatt.] Why would your minister say that we don't believe in his divinity, when we do?" I wasn't telling the full truth; I knew what she meant. She believed that Jesus was the second Person of the Blessed Trinity and equal to the Father in every way. The Witnesses believe that Jesus is a created god, a secondary god: divine, but certainly not God Almighty. Since I wanted to get her involved with us and place my literature in her home, I, without lying, gave her an evasive answer, one I hoped would satisfy her. I was using *theocratic tact* as I had been trained to do. I was overcoming her objection, brushing it aside.

Here is another example of theocratic tact. When someone would ask if we were trying to convert him, we had been taught to reply: "Oh, no, that's a personal decision. Our work is to inform people of the good news that God has established his kingdom in the heavens and that he will soon remove all suffering and death from the earth. This is the message we preach. Converting people is not our job, but God's! Wouldn't you like to know more about how God is going to bring about a paradise for all men?" This answer is, of course, dishonest, because we were trained to make disciples.[3]

One afternoon when I returned from field service, my partners told me that an F.B.I. agent had come to the house looking for me. At first they tried to scare me, and I thought they were joking. But they insisted that it was true. The agent had asked a lot of questions about what I was doing. The result was that a short time later I received a letter and card from the Selective Service (draft board) notifying me that I had been classified 4–D. This is the classification for clergymen in the United States. I was particularly happy about it, for it meant that I had received the same classification as a priest or a minister, and I wouldn't have to face a jail sentence for refusing military service. Before registering at the draft board in Santa Monica, the Witnesses had counseled me on what exemption to seek. I had filled out the conscientious objector forms, even though the Witnesses who counseled me explained that our application for exemption was on the grounds that we were ministers of the gospel. They explained that we did believe in war, God's war, the greatest of all wars, but we wouldn't be fighting it because the angels would do that for us. (We'd just get the booty when it was over.)

After almost a year in Houlton my money ran out. I had

[3] One of our training manuals, *Qualified to Be Ministers*, says: "The home Bible studies we hold with the people are not an objective in themselves. They are to be alive, moving, progressive, and held for the purpose of directing the sheep to the great ark of safety, the theocratic system of things, and to the organization now operating within it. . . . But they also need to see that Jehovah has an organization and that it is Scripturally conducted" (rev. ed., 1967, p. 215); also *Kingdom Ministry*, September 1983, "Presenting the Good News", article "With One Objective: Starting Bible Studies".

never liked Houlton or the area very much, because the people were "closed to the truth". So I decided to move farther north to Caribou, where I could get some part-time employment. This town had a lot of French-speaking people, many of whom lived along the road to Van Buren, on the Canadian border. I started out living with Charlie and Danny. They were pioneers from around Chicago, and they were living in an apartment over the Kingdom Hall on Water Street. We didn't have running water, so we had to fetch it from the neighbor downstairs. The neighbor was our congregation servant, Bill Bolt. By now, I was used to sponge baths, since we hadn't had a shower or bathtub in Houlton. We really appreciated it when a Witness family invited us to bathe once a week at their farm about a mile out of town. The Byrums were potato farmers and very generous people. They gave us part-time work during the spring planting and the fall harvest, and in the winter we worked in their potato house. This was on a railroad siding and where we graded and sacked the potatoes.

Charlie eventually decided to go home to Illinois, so Danny became my partner. He also became my best friend. Of course, we did everything together, and I don't remember ever having any bad arguments with him. He was a very good pioneer and an encouragement to me. Jehovah's Witnesses are usually of the highest moral character. They work hard at developing a follower mentality and learn to be "organization-minded". Eventually, Lina and Tilly Byrum invited us to live with them at their farm.

The Byrums were a bilingual family. Tilly was from an English Protestant family in New Brunswick, Canada, and Lina from a French Catholic family on the Gaspé Peninsula. French was spoken most of the time in the house when I lived with them. They had plenty of room, since their children had married and left home. This was a big change for us. We had a family now, and good food. Danny and I helped out on the farm, milking cows and working in the planting and harvest to earn our room and board. I came to love the Byrums and their children as my own family. Tilly used to get up early in the morning and read the Bible aloud to his wife. He would translate things for her and explain them. We had many good discussions. Lina didn't speak English very well, and her sister not at all. I lived almost four years with the Byrums. It was they who taught me to speak French.

During this time, we were studying *Your Will Be Done*.[4] This JW book interpreted prophecies from the Book of Daniel in the Old Testament. It compared the Cold War between the United States and the Soviet Union to the competition between the King of the North and the King of the South found in Daniel. The proliferation of nuclear weapons meant Armageddon was fast approaching. During the Cuban missile crisis, when everyone around us was worried about what might happen, we Witnesses naively believed that what we were studying was coming to pass before our eyes. Some of us were telling people that they had better "listen up". We were happy to give our door-step presentation based on 2 Timothy 3:1, "But know this, that in the last days critical times hard to deal with will be here" (NWT). We particularly liked those expressions "last days" and "critical times hard to deal with". We stressed them a lot. Since we believed ourselves to be the only people who understood the Bible, we had good reason to feel smug. We were Jehovah's people, and he was warning only us about what was going to happen in the near future.

After pioneering for five years in northern Maine, I had an appointment with someone who was going to influence my life in a very important manner. Dana Cushman was a deacon in the First Baptist Church of Caribou and respected for his knowledge of the Bible. He, too, was a potato farmer, and

[4] Brooklyn: WTBTS, 1958.

he was a friend of Tilly's son, Norman. Dana used to be Norman's Sunday-school teacher before Norman converted to the Jehovah's Witnesses. Norman explained to me how much he thought of Mr. Cushman, how sincere he was, and so on. He was so devout that he wouldn't harvest on Sunday, the Lord's Day. Norman asked me to meet with Dana and try to win him to the truth. I assured him that I would be happy to meet him. Since I was twenty-two and had been a pioneer for some time now, I thought I had enough experience to handle Dana.

How does a JW prepare for such a meeting? Does he fast, pray a lot, or what? Well, if he does anything, he studies a lot. We had a manual called *Make Sure of All Things*,[5] which classified 123 subjects and quoted the supporting Bible passages for each one. It also had a thorough index for cross-referencing many more topics. Using this book, I thought it best to review the subjects that would give me an advantage: soul, hell, and the Trinity. If I could prove that man didn't have an immortal soul, torment in hell would be out of the question. And if Dana got onto the Trinity, I would be ready for him. Besides, who could explain it? So I spent a lot of hours preparing and writing cross-references into my Bible. The meeting was scheduled for one afternoon. Dana arrived right on time. He seemed to be a pleasant fellow; he was about twenty years older than I.

We sat down together in Norman's kitchen. I began by asking him what subject he would like to discuss first. I expected him to say the Trinity or hell. But instead he placed a big copy of the King James Bible on the table between us and said, "I think that we ought to talk about what is most important." I couldn't object to that, so I said, "Okay, Mr. Cushman, what do *you* think is the most important subject?" Without hesitation he replied, "Jesus Christ and salvation."

[5] Rev. ed. (Brooklyn: WTBTS, 1957).

That surprised me, but I couldn't see how to avoid it, so I agreed to it.

I started by trying to show from the Scriptures that Jesus was created by God, inferior to the Father, and therefore subject to him. Dana gave me the usual arguments in return. We went round and round, each thinking he was right and that he was winning the debate. Dana was telling me that one had only to believe in Jesus Christ in order to be saved, and I was insisting that, according to James 2, faith wasn't enough, works also were required. Doesn't Scripture say that even the devil believes? I explained that to be saved one has to be a part of Jehovah's organization. He also has to take in "accurate knowledge" (1 Tim 2:5, NWT) and come to know Jehovah as "the only true God" and his son, Jesus (Jn 17:3). I tried attacking the Baptists and all the churches; I wanted to show how we were so different, so much better. To my surprise he didn't try to defend his denomination but, instead, kept his arguments focused on the Person of Jesus Christ.

Suddenly, he surprised me by seeming to agree with me. "Okay," he said, "there is one work necessary to be saved. Will you believe it if I show it to you from the Scriptures? Let's see what Jesus said about the only work necessary for salvation." I had a hard time following him on that. He had been arguing all along that works weren't necessary for salvation, and now he seemed to be compromising his position. What did he have up his sleeve; what was this work? Turning to John 6; he read verses 28 and 29, with me following along in my NWT.

> Therefore they said to him: "What shall we do to work the works of God?" In answer Jesus said to them: "This is the work of God, that you exercise faith in him whom that One sent forth" (NWT).

My jaw dropped, but nothing came out of my open mouth. For the first time since I had become a JW, I didn't have a ready answer. How could he take sides with me, agree with me that a work was necessary, and then turn it into *faith*? I was stunned. Since I had nothing more to say, we ended the discussion right then and there. Though he brought me to the Savior's feet, I was not ready to surrender, to accept Jesus as *my* Lord and *my* God (Jn 20:28). I would think about it later, however. Ten years later the Holy Spirit would cause me to remember our discussion, and I would recall everything that Dana Cushman, the Baptist deacon from Maine, had told me.

Ken teaching at Gilead School in Brooklyn, 1968

CHAPTER 5

Within the Watchtower

Not long after my meeting with Dana Cushman, Dennis Trumbore, the circuit servant for Maine, recommended Danny and me for service as special pioneers. We were assigned to the Houlton congregation of Jehovah's Witnesses. I was appointed overseer, and Danny was named the assistant overseer. Some time after we moved to Houlton, I was preaching from house to house and came upon the local Baptist minister. I gave him the same sermon I was trying to deliver at every door. His response was bold to say the least. He told me: "Young man, I want to challenge your heart for Jesus Christ. I am going to pray for you, and you are not going to rest until you come to know him and accept him as your personal Savior." He said this with such conviction that he made a very strong impression on me. I went away thinking about it. I couldn't get it out of my mind. When I went to bed that night, I asked Jehovah to protect me from demon influences. I was uneasy, especially after that encounter with Dana. Every crack and noise seemed to suggest the devil was invading my bedroom. I concluded that the minister was demonized, reminding myself that the clergy belong to the "man of sin" class. They are the most reprehensible because, in spite of their knowledge of the Bible, they hide the truth about Jehovah and his name from the poor people (the "Lazarus" class).[1] This is a normal JW

---

[1] Lk 16:22, 23; 2 Th 2:3 (KJV). This is typical JW talk. They love to describe different groups as typified by individuals in the Bible. According to the JWs, the rich man pictures the clergy, and the poor man, Lazarus,

reaction. The Witnesses are very afraid of the devil and his demons. When they meet a person with strong religious convictions, they often leave the door saying, "Did you see the look on her face? She is really demon-possessed!" Because they believe they are the only ones who have the truth, they think that other religious people must belong to the devil.

I wouldn't remain in Houlton for long. That same year, 1963, I attended the district convention in New York City and filled out the application forms for Bethel service. The leadership was stressing the growing need for young workers to come to headquarters in Brooklyn (called *Bethel*) and work in the printery and bindery. When I heard how important this was, I thought, if this is what Jehovah wants, I'll answer the call. (Danny also decided to enter into Bethel service.) Brooklyn would be a tremendous change from beautiful Maine. I thought I was making a great sacrifice. On the other hand, my new life might be better. I would be at the center of Jehovah's organization. It would be like serving God at the Vatican if one were a Catholic.

We were asked to read through the entire Bible before reporting for Bethel service by December 1, 1963. In those

<hr />

pictures the loyal remnant of the 144,000. When Christ came, the poor people's situation was reversed. The rich man (scribes, Sadducees, and Pharisees) lost his place and was tormented by the fire of Christ's preaching. The poor people, who previously had received nothing but crumbs from their clergy, were now received and comforted in Abraham's (God's) bosom. In the modern-day application of this parable, Christ came to rule in 1914, and, in 1918, to judge his people and the other religions. Since 1918 the remnant (remaining members of the 144,000) have received favor from God, and now they scorch the kingdom opposers (the clergy) by the fire of their preaching. This language and such interpretation of "classes" goes all the way back to the founder, C. T. Russell. See Edmond Charles Gruss, *Apostles of Denial: An Examination and Exposé of the History, Doctrines and Claims of the Jehovah's Witnesses* (Nutley, N.J.: Presbyterian and Reformed Publishing, 1970), pp. 228–29.

days, the Society[2] was inviting new Bethel members in groups of about twenty-five people. Such a group formed a class for a six-month training program called Primary School. We got to know one another well as we learned the ropes together. It helped to be with other newcomers, because we were green and often arriving late to the meal table or to work because we had to stop to ask directions.

At that time, two large buildings across the street from each other made up the Bethel Home, the lodgings for the workers. It was a ten-minute walk from there to the two factory buildings where most of us worked. I was assigned a room in the newer housing at 107 Columbia Heights. It was on the fifth floor, which was occupied by men only. Each room was shared by two men and contained two beds, a closet, a writing table, a bookcase and a wash basin. Our building was known as the Gilead building because the missionary school was located on the second floor. On the ground floor were the offices that directed the field service activities of the congregations and the pioneers in the United States. At 124 Columbia Heights, across the street from the Gilead building, was the other, older building containing the writing department and the offices of the Watchtower Society's president, vice president, and the secretary-treasurer. In the basement was a sauna and the laundry department. One dining room seated 543 people, the other 400. A third dining room was added later to seat 125 more. Both buildings had a library of the JW publications, along with biblical commentaries and other books. The two buildings were joined by an underground tunnel, so that people and equipment didn't need to cross the street above.

Here's a typical day at the headquarters of "God's organization". We awoke at 6:30 in the morning to the clanging of a bell. We ran down the hall to the showers, hoping one

---

[2] This expression, "the Society", usually refers to the leadership of the WTBTS.

would be available, and washed as quickly as possible. After dressing, we ran to the elevator. If it was full, we took the stairs, using the stainless steel banisters to leap four or six stairs at a time. We then ran through the tunnel to reach the dining rooms across the street by 7 A.M. Running through the place like this was frowned upon, but it seemed necessary in order to arrive anywhere on time. Punctuality was considered so important that it was unthinkable to arrive at breakfast even a minute late. Everyone dreaded the humiliation of having all eyes following him as he took a seat in the rear corner of the room and of having the table head warn him against making a bad reputation for himself.

After breakfast (7:25), it was time to leave for work. We had a five-and-one-half-day work week. We put in eight hours and forty minutes, with a break for lunch. On Saturdays, we worked four hours. We received our room and board for our labor and a monthly allowance of fourteen dollars to cover expenses.[3]

Many "new boys" started out in the bindery. One job in the bindery was very demanding physically. It involved manually placing newly covered books between heavy boards in tall presses to dry. These boards have metal edges, which under pressure make the groove you can see in any hardbound book. Sometimes one who "messed up" would be assigned to the bindery as punishment. Others were sent there to be tested, to see how humble and persevering they were. Years later, a Witness friend in California asked me if I might

[3] It is worth noting that during the Second World War, draftees who did alternate service in the Civilian Public Service Camps received fifteen dollars per month "maintenance wage". See Melvin Gingerich, "Discipleship Expressed in Alternate Service", in *The Recovery of the Anabaptist Vision*, ed. Guy F. Hershberger (Scottsdale, Penn.: Herald Press, 1957), p. 267. A couple of years later, because of rising subway fares, the Society gave us a number of subway tokens each month in order to avoid raising allowances in other branches around the world.

talk to her son about leaving Bethel. He was working in the bindery, she said, and he had grown so thin that she was worried about his health.

I was spared working in the bindery. I was twenty-three years old when I entered Bethel, with five years experience in the pioneer service. Perhaps it was thought that I was mature enough. In any case, I was sent to work in the job-press department on the seventh floor of the factory building at 117 Adams Street. There I helped the operator of a large paper cutter and packaged and boxed the handbills we sent out to congregations across the country. It was not a mentally stimulating job, but I liked the men with whom I worked. Also, the factory was an interesting place. At one end of the floor were thirty-two linotype machines (used for typesetting) and the composition department. The opposite end of the floor is where workers nickelplated the curved plates for the eighteen rotary printing presses. These presses were able to print twenty-five thousand magazines per hour. They used up a five-mile-long sixteen-hundred-pound roll of paper in about forty minutes. At that time the Witnesses were producing literature in 146 languages.

Our evenings after dinner were spent in meetings and classes. Monday night was reserved for the Bethel family's study of *The Watchtower*. We all gathered at 7:30 in the Kingdom Hall located at the 107 building. After studying the lesson for the coming Sunday, I went to the Primary School class (only for new people), and when it was finished I went to the library to study and prepare homework.

Once the Primary School was completed, we were able to join the rest of the "family" in the Theocratic Ministry School that was a part of the program at Bethel. This gave us an opportunity to know the older, more mature members and benefit from either hearing or receiving counsel from them. At this point the new members received their assignments to a congregation in the greater New York City area. I was privileged to receive an appointment as a book study conductor in the Bethel congregation. My territory was the famous Greenwich Village in New York City.

After I was at Bethel about a year, I was transferred to a job on the ninth floor of the same factory building, where there was a hand-bindery department with several stitching and folding machines for booklets and magazines. On this floor up to one hundred thousand thirty-two page booklets could be stitched in a day. I was made the overseer (supervisor) for this floor. In a side office, I had a little Multilith offset duplicator for printing jobs that the Society considered confidential. This press also served for short-run letters that didn't need to go to the job-press department. Our crew, as well as the jobs we did, would vary a lot. I liked this variety and the detailed handwork we did.

Our normal crew consisted of about five people, and we got to know each other well. When things were slow, we rebound books for the Bethel and Gilead libraries. Because of the calendar production for the coming year, work increased around November, so I called in volunteers from outside Bethel. These were usually young pioneer women. This is when our department really hummed, with up to sixty people on the floor. When we prepared for the summer conventions, we had students from all over the world working in our department. They came to attend the Watchtower's Bible School of Gilead for missionaries. This school was founded in 1942 and opened with its first class in February 1943. The Society brought in two groups of one hundred students each year for training. One had to have at least two years' experience as a full-time pioneer in order to qualify. Most students also studied a foreign language. Some of the students would eventually be made responsible for entire countries. Working with them gave me the opportunity to meet highly qualified people from other lands.

During my time in Bethel, I witnessed the expansion of the work. I saw a new factory building go up across the street. It was ten stories high and covered two hundred thousand square feet. Later, when in Africa, I heard about the acquisition of the giant Squibb pharmaceutical properties just down the street from the Bethel Home. The JWs got ten buildings in one purchase. But this would be only the beginning, as they would continue to expand, buying hotels and property to lodge more workers.

Neighbors didn't like seeing all these young people crowding the sidewalks, even though we were an earnest, clean-cut group. Still, some Bethel workers had problems adjusting. For example, a couple of young fellows went up to the roof to drink, got drunk, and vomited on the roof. They were called before the entire Bethel family to be publicly disciplined. One was sent home, and the other was put on probation at Bethel. Newcomers learned about it when others pointed him out and told the story. Of course, he was sent to the standing presses in the bindery. A few years later, a ring of homosexuals was broken up; some of them had occupied important positions in headquarters. One of the young men in my class was a peeping Tom. Several times the police pursued him right to the very door of the Bethel Home.

"Will you be alive in 75?" was a jingle we began singing around the factory after the 1966 summer conventions. The phrase was our response to a publication released that year: *Life Everlasting—In Freedom of the Sons of God.*[4] The first chapter contains a timeline, described as a "trustworthy Bible chronology". It gave 4,026 B.C. as the date when Adam was created and 1975 as the completion of six thousand years of man's history. The book claimed that the seventh "prophetic day" is the millennium, a one-thousand-year-long Sabbath

[4] Brooklyn: WTBTS, 1966.

rest for mankind. It would be a rest "day", following the biblical idea that says that God rested on the seventh day. "How appropriate it would be for Jehovah God to make of this coming seventh period of a thousand years a Sabbath period of rest and release, a great Jubilee Sabbath for the proclaiming of liberty throughout the earth to all its inhabitants" (p. 29). Of course, the only inhabitants remaining on earth would be Jehovah's Witnesses; everyone else would be destroyed at Armageddon.

Such statements as "trustworthy Bible chronology"[5] and "the short time remaining"[6] used in the Society's publications were enough to stir the Witnesses to a greater effort. We truly believed that the end of the old world and the beginning of the new world was imminent. Some incurred debts they never intended to pay. Others sold their homes and went into full-time service. The *Kingdom Ministry* in 1974 exhorted JWs with these words:

> A 34–percent increase! Does that not warm our hearts? Reports are heard of brothers selling their homes and property and planning to finish out the rest of their days in this old system in the pioneer service. Certainly this is a fine way to spend the short time remaining before the wicked world's end—1 John 2:17.[7]

The following year, Vice President Fred Franz announced at the JW convention in Los Angeles that Witnesses should forego higher education, marriage, and children, because "the time does not allow for that, dear friends. . . . Evidently there is not much time left." A 1975 issue of *Kingdom Ministry* explained that even "a decision to pursue a career in this

[5] *Life Everlasting*, p. 29.

[6] "How Are You Using Your Life?", *Kingdom Ministry*, May 1974, p. 3. *Kingdom Ministry* is a service sheet passed out only to people who attend the Service Meeting of Jehovah's Witnesses.

[7] Ibid.

system of things is not only unwise but extremely dangerous."[8]

Remarks such as these are powerful stuff for those who
follow an organization they believe to be directed by God
himself. The Watchtower Society has a long-standing tradition of warning its followers that the end is near. They have
taught for some time that 1914 was a turning point in world
history, that the First World War was visible proof that
Christ had begun ruling and that the devil had intensified
his struggle to mislead all mankind. Many books chronicling
the Witnesses' false prophetic speculations are readily available.[9]

During the summer of 1968, we received another book
that would be highly useful in our preaching work. It was a
small blue book that many referred to as the *blue bomb*. The
name of the book? *The Truth That Leads to Eternal Life*.[10] As of
this writing, 107,553,888 copies have been printed in 117
languages.[11] It has twenty-two chapters, and the Watchtower
Society instructed us to try to study the entire book with our
students in just six months.[12] Why only six months? Because
of the *short time remaining* before Armageddon, we were told
not to waste time with people who, after having received

[8] For quotations, Edmond C. Gruss, *The Jehovah's Witnesses and Prophetic
Speculation*, 2d ed. (Nutley, N.J.: Presbyterian and Reformed Pub., 1975).
See particularly chap. 4 and the appendix beginning on p. 96.

[9] Duane Magnani with Arthur Barrett, *The Watchtower Files* (Minneapolis: Bethany House, 1985), chap. 8. Raymond Franz, *Crisis of Conscience*
(Atlanta: Commentary Press, 1983), chap. 9.

[10] Brooklyn: WTBTS, 1966. For the official story by Jehovah's Witnesses concerning the importance of these two books (*Life Everlasting—in
Freedom of the Sons of God* and *The Truth That Leads to Eternal Life*) and the
year 1975, see: *Jehovah's Witnesses—Proclaimers of God's Kingdom* (Brooklyn: WTBTS, 1993), pp. 104–5.

[11] *Jehovah's Witnesses—Proclaimers of God's Kingdom*, p. 594 (this page has
a photo of the book); see p. 571 for a picture of the home Bible Study.

[12] *1975 Yearbook of Jehovah's Witnesses,* French ed. (Brooklyn, WTBTS,
1975), p. 239.

sufficient instruction, were not demonstrating any progress toward becoming Jehovah's Witnesses.

The statistics found in the *1975 Yearbook of Jehovah's Witnesses* furnish some important clues as to the leadership's motives for the release of the blue bomb two years after the publication of *Life Everlasting*. From 1960 to 1965, the annual rate of baptisms worldwide stood at about 60,000, but in 1966 they dropped to 58,904. The 1966 speculation that the world *could* end in 1975, coupled with the 1968 release of the blue bomb, caused the number of publishers (i.e., JWs) to increase substantially. Referring to the blue bomb, one leader claimed, "There is no disputing that Jehovah has produced this small but powerful instrument for making disciples."[13] The *Truth* book was designed for a six-months' Bible study.

When questioned about this, Jehovah's Witnesses will make excuses for their leaders. Why? Because they are unable to envision any alternative to their religion. They have given so much and worked so hard, that they can't face up to the possibility that they might have misplaced their trust. Some JWs have told me that, should they ever discover they have been wrong, they will simply live for themselves and have nothing more to do with any religion.

I often wondered when, how, and if I would get married. I had signed a contract upon applying for service at the headquarters that I would remain single for four years if I were accepted. One day, a young Gilead student from Quebec was assigned to work in my department. Others had already spoken to me about this young, slim, French-speaking student. They knew I spoke French because I often served as a tour guide for visitors from France. Since I had been asked to tu-

---

[13] Ibid., p. 240; for the increase in publishers, see *Jehovah's Witnesses—Proclaimers of God's Kingdom*, p. 105, par. 3–4. "Coming as it did at a time when there was a feeling of expectancy and urgency among Jehovah's Witnesses, the Truth book and the six-month Bible study campaign greatly aided in speeding up the disciple-making work" (par. 4).

tor the students learning French, I had more opportunities to mix with the students, and with Monique in particular, who also was helping her fellow students to learn French. Monique, her Canadian friends, and I visited a lot. I used to walk through the library in the evenings just to say hello.

At the time, I was serving as a book study conductor for a French-speaking group in a congregation that had a large number of Haitian immigrants in its territory. Our assignment was to visit only people who spoke French in order to direct them to our congregation, which used French in all its meetings. I asked Monique to accompany me in the field service, and she was happy to join me. As time went on, I became very attached to her. I decided it was time to seek some advice from an older brother, George Gangas.[14] George was the instructor for the French class and so a collaborator and a friend.[15] What did he think of my getting involved with Monique, I asked. I expected him to tell me that I shouldn't get involved, that I should give myself completely to Bethel service, just as he had done. So I was quite surprised when he recommended that I pursue my interest in Monique. He told me he admired her and thought that she was a very humble person. I could hardly believe what I was hearing. He didn't say it with any bitterness or as if he had regrets over his decision to remain single and spend his life at Bethel. He simply said: "Go ahead; don't stay here. Get married."

I had been at Bethel for four years and had kept my promise to remain single. So I took Brother Gangas' advice and began dating Monique. We still had the summer and a few extra months while she waited for her visa to enter the Ivory Coast (the missionary assignment she had received). Just be-

[14] His picture appears on p. 260 in *Jehovah's Witnesses—Proclaimers of God's Kingdom*.

[15] He was also one of the "anointed", so a member of the 144,000 chosen for heaven.

fore she left, I wanted to ask her to marry me. But she wouldn't let me pop the question; she had promised to be a missionary, and she wanted to follow through with her vocation. Besides, as she explained to me later, it would give her a chance to sort out her feelings.

I was devastated after her departure. We had grown so close; I felt lost without her. For several weeks, I walked around so alone, so sad. I knew I had to write and ask her to marry me. Waiting for her reply was terrible. In fact, she never got the proposal letter I sent her. I was under so much stress that I wrote her postal box number incorrectly. I began losing weight as I anxiously waited for an answer. Why didn't she mention my proposal in her letters? Finally a letter came, saying: "If you mean what I think you mean, the answer is yes." Was I elated! I passed from the "pits" to the heavens. One morning, I was thinking about Monique while preparing my cereal. Someone asked me what I was doing. Why was I pouring coffee on my cereal? People were becoming suspicious that perhaps I was engaged, that my days at Bethel were numbered.

I realized that in order to marry Monique I would have to become a missionary and go to Africa. I had heard from some missionaries that on a visit to an African village they had been invited to eat rodent. I didn't see how I would be able to do that! However, I took courage one morning after breakfast and approached the Society's president: "Brother Knorr," I said, "I would like to go to Gilead (missionary school) because I have just become engaged to Monique Bolduc." (I was obligated to do this in order to join Monique in Africa.) Upon learning that I had fulfilled my contract at Bethel (four years), Knorr said: "Send me your request in writing." Not long afterward, I received a letter accepting me into Gilead for the term beginning on April 22, 1968. I was told to begin reading the Old Testament before the term commenced. Monique had been a student in the forty-sixth class, and I would be a student in the forty-eighth class of Gilead. (The forty-seventh class was already filled.)

Gilead courses were geared to learning the Bible and methods of teaching and preaching. Like the previous classes, one hundred students were called in for this class. The School's program was arranged in the following manner. The students were divided into four groups of twenty-five students. Fifty of them (call them group A) went to classes in the morning, while the other fifty (group B) worked in the factories. The following day, they alternated, so that group A went to work in the afternoons and group B went to classes. This provided exercise for the students and cheap labor for the factories. This also made good use of the limited classroom space.

This is the manner in which we studied a book of the Bible. The book was divided into a number of sections and distributed among the students, who were organized into study groups of three or four persons. Then each group researched and prepared an assignment. When this work was finished, a student was called upon to stand in front of a class of twenty-five students and present his report. The student gave the results of his research with the necessary references to *Watchtower* and *Awake!* magazines or any other JW publications consulted. The instructor listened from his desk. If he thought there was something to add or correct, he would do so. When the reports were finished, he gave his own summary and covered any points that had been missed. This was the time to pay close attention, because we would be tested on the material the next day.

Our studies and the preparation of our papers often kept us busy until midnight. Frankly, it was a tough schedule, similar to a crash course. We teamed up with other students with whom we built friendships to quiz and help each other. My roommate was Danish. We often had a German couple come to our room to study with us over a bowl of Fritos,

cheese and Tabasco sauce, and beer. A couple of evenings a
week, I tutored students in the French language. I even had
the privilege of teaching the French class in the instructor's
absence.

Saturday mornings we had one-and-one-half hour lectures on Bible topics and on the culture and history of nations and civilizations. We had to learn the laws of ancient
Israel and how to apply them to present-day situations. We
prepared skits for class discussion. After a skit, the students
asked questions or pointed out faults. Some Saturday afternoons the Gilead students were given tours of important
places in New York, such as the United Nations, the New
York Metropolitan Museum of Art, and the American Museum of Natural History.

For doctrinal study, my class used the books *Things in
Which It Is Impossible for God to Lie*[16] and *Life Everlasting—In
Freedom of the Sons of God*. We went straight through these
publications in class. We had a course called Theocratic Ministry, in which we learned how to sit for interviews on television, how to hold a microphone, and so on. We drew
sketches of the best layouts for organizing interviews.

Students did not receive grades. We were judged silently,
secretly. We had frequent tests and final exams that were very
complete. At graduation time, everyone filed up to receive
his envelope. Upon opening it, he discovered if he had
earned a diploma or not. This avoided any public embarrass-
ment. If his grade averages were not sufficiently high, a student didn't receive a diploma, but he still could be assigned as
a missionary or maybe return to pioneer work.

Graduation was an important event, and many people
were invited. Students who could sing or play musical instru-
ments prepared entertainment. I am not at all gifted in music,
so I was given a small role in a drama on Belshazzar's feast,

[16] Brooklyn: WTBTS, 1966.

recounted in the Book of Daniel. We spent a lot of Saturdays practicing for it, and the students made costumes. It was a fun event, especially for me, because I was looking forward to seeing Monique soon afterward.

After graduation, I returned to work at the factory in my old department. While waiting for my visa, I got the required shots (yellow fever and smallpox) for entering the Ivory Coast. I fretted about the possibility that the visa might not be granted. I had learned that each year the Witnesses in the Ivory Coast worried about getting a renewal permit for their work. There had been a problem in the past over a Witness who had killed someone in a fight, and it had caused a riot and attacks on the Witnesses by members of the dead man's tribe. As a consequence, the Witnesses were banned for a time. *The Watchtower* was also banned in the Ivory Coast, probably because it was a former colony of France, where the magazine was also prohibited. The Witnesses in the Ivory Coast got around this by publishing *The Watchtower* under a different title: *La Sentinelle*. In France, they issued the main articles in a small journal called *Le Bulletin intérieur*, which they distributed only to members and to people who regularly attended their meetings.

Before leaving New York, I received a letter from Brother Knorr, the Society's president, informing us I would have to wait a year in the mission work as a single person before I could marry. This shows how much we were under the Society's thumb. Witnesses criticize Catholics for having a celibate priesthood, but they required me to promise four years of celibate life in order to enter Bethel and then to postpone marriage for another year after that. Of course, being a faithful JW, I accepted these arrangements. The important thing was to get married; another year wouldn't change anything. It meant a two-year engagement period would be necessary; hard, but not impossible.

Ken, at far left, as Jehovah's Witness missionary in the Ivory Coast

CHAPTER 6

A Missionary to the Ivory Coast

Finally the long-awaited day of departure arrived. I traveled to the Ivory Coast with three other missionaries, whom I had tutored in French. The flight from New York to Abidjan took about eighteen hours. When we landed in Dakar, Senegal, to refuel, I couldn't get over the excitement. Here I was, at last, in Africa, another continent! I stepped out of the air-conditioned plane and was shocked by the heat and humidity. It felt as if someone had thrown a wet, hot blanket over me. Not even the warm, muggy summers of New York City had prepared me for the climate here.

When we landed in Abidjan (population 450,000 in 1968), the capital of the Ivory Coast, we discovered a beautiful, modern city, where the old met the new. A welcoming committee composed of missionaries and Witnesses from Treichville and Adjamé were waving and yelling "*Bonne arrivée, frère*", "*Bonne arrivée, soeurs*". Among them were the Adjamé home servant and his wife, who were English Canadians from Quebec. I already knew them, because they had gone though an earlier Gilead class. Best of all, my fiancée, Monique, was there. I hadn't seen her for a year, but the separation had, indeed, made our hearts grow fonder.

Since I had saved my vacation time, I spent the next two weeks in the company of Monique, getting to know Abidjan and its beaches. The city has its popular neighborhoods, such as Treichville and Adjamé, but the town's center, called Plateau, has a beautiful park and is as modern and pretty as Santa Monica. The city hall could compete with any in the world, and there were two cinemas and an African open-air market that sold practically anything you needed. On the edge of the lagoon was the Hotel Ivoire, with a swimming pool and a casino.

There are sixty-five languages and dialects spoken in the Ivory Coast. The main native languages I heard were Dioula, Baoulé, and Beté. The country also has a large number of immigrants from Upper Volta (Burkina Faso, today), Ghana, Dahomey, Togo, and Nigeria. The country's major exports are coffee, cacao, and timber.

After my vacation and tearful good-byes, I took the train for my missionary assignment in Bouaké, the second largest city in the country. The trip took almost all day, since the train had to go slowly in some places. I was fascinated by all the bright colors and the new things I was seeing. The native cloth (called *pagne* in French) was used for women's dresses and men's shirts. It was of many colors and had a variety of prints or designs. Often the Ivoirians wore nothing more than a simple cloth wrapped around the body. It hung from the waist or from just above the breast. Whenever the train stopped, young men and women of all ages flocked to the sides of the train to sell oranges, bananas, and shish kebabs to the passengers. They also offered palm wine (*bangui*), which we were warned not to drink. We were instructed to boil or filter our drinking water and to soak all vegetables and lettuce in a mixture of bleach and water to kill amoebas.

I planned to go as often as possible to Abidjan to visit Monique. Traveling meant losing two days of field service, so I was obliged to make up some of that time with her when on a visit. When I accompanied her to any Bible studies she conducted, she would ask me to lead the study. This was necessary because JW women are not allowed to conduct a study in the presence of a man; if, for some reason, she should do so, she must cover her head with a hat or kerchief to signify that she is in her proper place (submissive to male leadership).[1] JWs insist on this because they consider the Bible study to be an extension of the Christian congregation. Monique was tireless, a hard worker in the home and in the field service. She trotted up and down hills, along footpaths, all over town. The weather and the busy schedule seemed to tire me more than her. On one of my visits, I just didn't have the strength to keep up with her. I wondered if I had a touch of malaria or something, but I was embarrassed to ask her to slow down.

Sometimes Monique came to visit me in Bouaké. We spent some late night hours on the porch, hardly talking, just enjoying being together. Monique would take my bedroom during her visit, and I would sleep on the tile floor in the dining room.

This visiting was a drain on our personal budgets. We often traveled by train in the second-class coach, but sometimes, to save money, we traveled third class, surrounded by Africans carrying live chickens and market produce. It wasn't easy; just getting on board was a shoving and pushing match. The organization gave us room and board and seven dollars a month for personal expenses. Dating and traveling on this small allowance required being a magician. Therefore our literature placements (sales) were very important to us. Literature purchases at missionary rates cost practically nothing, and so we made a profit on book sales.

Missionaries in different homes around the world no doubt followed the same routine we did. New missionaries were required to spend the first month studying the language. The second month they divided their time between field service and language study. After that, they were in field service full time and were expected to continue working on improving their language skills. Since I was already proficient in French, the official language, I could go straight to work.

---

[1] JWs base this practice on 1 Cor 11:4–16; 14:34.

The missionary team already in Bouaké consisted of an English couple and two single men, a German and a Canadian. The Englishman, Dave, was in charge of the missionary home, the rented villa in which we lived. I was lucky to have a room to myself; the other two fellows shared a room. The mission home also served as a meeting place, which meant that three times a week it became our Kingdom Hall. About twenty people were already coming to meetings, including two Witness families, one from Dahomey and another from Togo. The size of the group was largely due to Otto, the German, who had been very successful making disciples. He seemed to be good at impressing the people and was strict with them. He warned his students that, if they didn't keep their appointments, they would go to the end of the line for studies with him. He was always interested to know how many books and magazines I had placed by the end of the month. He had usually been top man in literature placements before I arrived. His attitudes inclined us to believe that he had ambitions of becoming a circuit or district servant.

I had house duty one day a week and one weekend a month. On those days I had to be well-organized to meet my daily goal of five hours in field service. I got up before the others to prepare breakfast. Then I served the table. The others seemed to delight in remarking that I had forgotten the salt or sugar or some other item, so that I would have to get up. Before breakfast, just as in Brooklyn, we had our discussion of the text for the day, taken from the current *Yearbook*. After breakfast, I cleared the table, washed dishes, and got the old wringer washing machine going for my clothes. After they were washed, I hung them out to dry and then walked to the open-air market about a half a kilometer from our house. I would buy a load of oranges, because we drank a lot of juice every day. Then I made a tour of the market to see what I needed; we usually bought our meat in the African market because it was cheaper there. Sometimes I went to the European market, which was the size of a small American corner grocery store and about a half kilometer from the outdoor market, to see if I could get tomato sauce or some other ingredient for the day's meal. Then, all loaded up, I walked home. We were allowed to take a taxi or get a "boy" to help us only when absolutely necessary. We were frugal, because we were expected to get the best deals and to economize with Jehovah's money.

Back home, I prepared the dinner and popped it into the oven. I quickly learned that throwing some soup over the meat and vegetables made for an easy meal. The beef we bought was tough and needed a lot of stewing, so, while it was in the oven, I attended to my other work, such as studying and preparing public conferences or assignments for the Ministry School and Service Meeting. After I set the table and called the others, we had prayer and ate. I served the table, cleared it, and washed dishes. I then turned to my ironing. By three or maybe four o'clock in the afternoon, I could spend a couple of hours making back calls or conducting a Bible study.

I had a larger territory in a part of town called Sokra. It was inhabited mostly by Moslem immigrants from Upper Volta and Mali, and I knew absolutely nothing of their dialect. This quarter was very poor. The houses were basically of cement blocks with tin roofs. Conducting a Bible discussion or study in one of these was impossible when it was raining.

The first time I went door to door in Sokra, I was accompanied by an African pioneer visiting friends in Bouaké for the weekend. When I say *door*, I am not describing anything like a door in America. No, the entrance to these houses was through a door that opened up into a courtyard. Around the courtyard were individual doors or dwellings, with a piece of cloth or bamboo hung to keep out the flies but to allow the air to pass. Other individual houses were like the circular mud houses you see in films of Africa. Stepping into the courtyard, or up to a door if no one was already cooking outside, we would just call out "*Ko, ko, ko*" or clap our hands together while crying out "*Ko, ko, ko.*" At the first residence, a woman answered our call, and I began introducing us in French. She said a couple of words to us that I couldn't understand. Turning to Boniface, I said, "Okay, you explain why we are here." He told me he didn't understand her either. I was really surprised, since he was an African. Then he explained that he wasn't from the Ivory Coast. I thought to myself, "What a poor partner he is." The woman began making some gestures, touching her ears and her mouth and clapping her hands together. I learned that this meant "I don't hear you", i.e., "I don't understand you."

This was a response I was going to see every day during the next seven months. It was a gesture I myself would use probably twenty times a day. This caused me to muse over how much time I wasted simply trying to communicate. Since I spent about three hours or more in the morning going door to door, I continually encountered illiterate women who were home doing the cooking. I asked myself, "Is this missionary work?" I am just putting in time to satisfy requirements. Jim, the Canadian missionary, or "Jacques", as we called him, was a big encouragement to me in the work. He liked this territory and was trying to learn Dioula.[2] I tried learning a few phrases from the Togolese Witness woman who was a vendor in the market. Jacques and I wrote the phrases down and practiced them. The most important phrase I learned was: "That's too expensive." Because we

---

[2] Dioula [sometimes spelled Dyoula] is very similar to Bambara, so I bought a book in Bambara to help me learn Dioula. These two languages belong to the same language group—*Mandingue*—which is spread over West Africa. Dioula is important because it is a *lingua franca*, a language used in the Ivory Coast by people who travel and those who sell in the markets.

were white, we were expected to pay more for anything the Africans had to sell.

The missionaries who were already there before me had naturally selected the more educated parts of town for their evangelism work. I complained to them that I had been as-signed the worst (meaning, you couldn't sell anything there) territory, and I wanted a piece of something else, something more productive. So I was made responsible for the territory where the railroad employees lived. This proved to be more interesting, because the people there were educated and had money. I could sell my books and expect to make return vis-its on those who had purchased them. The goal was always to establish a Bible study with the person and endeavor to win him to our beliefs. Eventually, I had twenty-five Bible studies in progress. These were more interesting than door-to-door work and meant I didn't have to walk so much under the blazing sun. (The Ivory Coast is only four degrees north of the Equator, and none of us had a car.)

One of the problems I faced was that many of the young people lacked any sense of time. But they didn't like to say no to the white man. I would make a rendezvous with someone who said he would come to my house, but I would then be obliged to spend an hour waiting for the person, who often wouldn't show up at all. This caused me to lose time and feel frustrated. Sometimes I would meet the person a week later in the street and ask him why he had missed the appoint-ment. He always had a good story to explain it.

Another problem we encountered was the fact that we stood out among a native population. This made us easily identifiable. No white men went door to door except JW missionaries. Once we had visited an area a time or two, the people knew who we were. I remember trying to walk dis-creetly down a street where I wanted to make some calls and then seeing a bunch of little kids staring at me. Before I got close they began chanting: "*Blafoué, Blafoué*" (white man, or

European, in Baoulé) or "*Toubabou, toubabou*" (the same in Dioula). When I approached them, they ran away. Then I knew I wouldn't find many people at home.

CHAPTER 7

Catastrophe Strikes

I had been in the Ivory Coast for about seven months, when, on a return trip by train to Bouaké, I ate a liver shish kebab and afterward was so thirsty that I drank some *bangui* the vendors were selling to the travelers. Somewhere, during or before this trip, I picked up a virus that would change my life forever. Too bad nobody thought to inquire whether we had been vaccinated for polio. Looking back, it appears that this is typical of the leadership, so perfectionist when it suits them, yet often careless in other areas. Maybe they considered polio a child's disease and took it for granted that adults had already been vaccinated. But that is not a legitimate excuse, because a doctor worked for them at Bethel, and many Jehovah's Witnesses are doctors. Some (including a former Bethel Service Department worker) have accused the headquarters of having gone so far as to falsify vaccination certificates because of their aversion to blood.

The Friday after this last trip to Abidjan, I began feeling very weak. The following Sunday afternoon, while Jacques and I were playing *Mil Bornes*, a French card game, I noticed stiffness in my neck and a pain in my lower back. Jacques and the others said to take a couple of aspirins. After I had taken as many as I dared, I still didn't feel any better, so I went to bed. As I lay in bed all day with a low fever, I kept thinking I had malaria, since the home servant was sick in bed with it. During the night, I got up to go to the bathroom. Because I felt so weak and not able to walk well, I followed the wall, leaning on it as I went. When I tried to urinate, practically nothing passed. (I was surprised, because I had been drinking quite a lot.) The next morning I made an effort to get out of bed, but my legs wouldn't move. I rolled over onto my side, and, pushing with my arms, I managed to sit up. I called the others and explained my problem. Someone left to get a male nurse who was a friend of the missionaries, and he came with his car and rushed me to the hospital for an examination.

Our African friend carried me into the hospital to see the French doctor on duty. A number of people were waiting in the hallway for their turn to see him. But the nurse went directly to the doctor and informed him of my condition. He saw me immediately. I was placed on the examination table, and the doctor began his exploration, touching me here and there with a needle to test my reactions. I had never heard the word poliomyelitis in French, but when the doctor said it aloud, I gasped. How could this happen *to me*, to Jehovah's faithful missionary? And I was to marry in six months. My legs were paralyzed, and the polio was progressing upward. Everyone worried about it reaching my lungs. I thought, "If I die, I'll wake up in paradise." But I didn't want to leave Monique: I wanted to get married and serve Jehovah with her. Paradise could wait! (I was no different from the Catholics I had criticized for not being in a rush to go to heaven!)

Monique arrived from Abidjan along with the Crawfords, who stayed at our house in Bouaké. The doctor told Monique to get vaccinated right away because of her contact with me. Immediately, Monique showed the kind of person she is. She saw that I received good care. She constantly had to run after the nurses to see that I got the necessary vitamin B shots. Polio is an attack on the motor nerves in the spine, and vitamin B is given to strengthen them.

My six-week stay in the Bouaké hospital was during the war in Biafra, and medicines were scarce, sometimes even past their expiration date. The doctor recommended that we buy our medicines in the pharmacy. I had exactly twelve dollars in the bank and no health insurance. The Society didn't carry insurance on us. Who was going to pay the bills? My friends talked to the doctor, who talked to the hospital administration. The Witnesses ended up not paying a cent for my medical care. So the world's "present system of things", which the Witnesses so severely criticize, was not so bad after all. In fact, the Witnesses continually ask for help from the world, even though they condemn it as evil and under Satan's control. Confined to a bed, I was not even able to see outdoors—the windows had wood louvers on them that allowed the light to shine in but prevented me from seeing outside. I had time to ponder such questions as: How could this happen to me? Wasn't I an important person in God's plan to bring the good news to the Ivoirian people? How would they survive Armageddon if I didn't bring them *into the truth*, into the ark of safety? Finally, I remembered this Scripture passage: "Time and unforeseen occurrence befall them all" (Ecc 9:11, NWT). I had to admit that God had nothing to do with it, and it was just one of those things. But why hadn't the Society been more vigilant in these matters?

Finally, the responsible brothers recognized that in order to receive adequate care I would have to leave the Ivory Coast. It was decided that I should go to Paris. I left the hospital in an ambulance that took me to the Abidjan airport. As I was lifted into the ambulance on a stretcher, I though how nice it was to feel the warmth of the sun and to see the beautiful sky, and I was truly saddened to be leaving this beautiful country. In the airplane my stretcher was fastened over six seats. How happy I was to have Monique accompany me on the flight. This was the time when the missionaries had a paid trip home to their respective countries so they could attend an international convention. Because of me, Monique received permission to leave a couple of weeks early.

At the Paris airport, Cesar Wawro, a French district servant, came to meet us. I already knew him well, because he had attended Gilead school a few years earlier. He accompanied the ambulance and made the necessary arrangements to get me admitted to the hospital in Garches, a suburb of Paris. This would be my home for six long months. I was alone in a strange country. I even had a hard time understanding Parisian French. The hospital personnel used a lot of slang. Even the words for some dishes were strange. When they brought our supper, they said: "Do you want some *ratatouille*?" "What's that?" I asked. "Can I smell it?" (I didn't like the sound of *rat* in the word!) The first time they asked if I wanted "jumped" potatoes—*les pommes de terre sautées*—I laughed. I couldn't imagine what they meant. Why couldn't they just say "fried potatoes"—*patates frites*—as they do in Quebec or in Maine?

I was placed in a *salle,* or ward, which had about eight other patients. The person across from me was a priest. He had caught polio in the Central African Republic when he was forty-eight years old. He was much worse off than I. He needed help to eat, to dress, for everything. Strange as it may seem, I was encouraged to see that he was in a worse condition than I. One man in our ward was so depressed that he jumped out of our third-floor window! I had eaten breakfast with him just that morning.

Monique was able to spend about ten days in Paris before she left to attend the 1969 international convention in New York. While in the States, she was able to meet my parents and my little sister (half-sister), who was born after I had gone to Maine. They were visiting in Rhode Island. She gave them the details of what had happened to me and brought them up to date. Afterward, they drove her to Montreal, where she spent the remainder of her vacation with her family. When her vacation was finished, Monique flew to Paris on her way back to the Ivory Coast.

How happy I was to see the one I loved. We spent each

Monique and Ken, during his recuperation from polio, Paris 1969

afternoon together during her stay. We were even taken to the JW convention then in progress in Paris. She got an appointment with the Society's president, Brother Knorr, who was also at the convention. He gave her a choice: she could stay in Paris as a special pioneer while she waited to see what kind of recovery I would have, or she could return to the Ivory Coast. Of course, he reminded her that she had promised to be a missionary, and he seemed to imply that I might not be able to be the kind of husband she needed. She decided to return to the Ivory Coast, something I understood, because Jehovah and his organization always have first place in our lives.

During the first few weeks in Paris, I did only simple exercises in a tub of hot water. As I lay in the tub, the therapist held my foot and told me to move it. Next I was to bend my knee, then move each leg to the right and then to the left. Later on, the therapist offered a little resistance to my movements. As I gained strength, he increased his resistance. When it was possible to weigh me, the scales showed I was a mere ninety-nine pounds. I spent most of the day listening to the radio, reading, or playing cards with other patients. I also read a small Protestant Bible I had with me.

Finally, I was fitted with a brace for my left leg, which was the weaker, and I began learning to walk again between two parallel bars. An elastic band was attached to a belt at my waist and tied to the left toe of my shoe so that the foot wouldn't point down or drag and make me stumble and fall. When I began walking outdoors, the aide did not always pay enough attention as he walked along behind me holding a belt that was attached to my waist. I took some great spills, falling stiffly straight forward like a tree. I would go down on my face, arms spread out before me. The positive side of my stay was that I rapidly improved in the French language. I never spoke English while I was there. People called me *Monsieur l'Américain* or, in slang, *l'amerloque*. I lost most of the Canadian accent I had acquired in Maine.

After six months, I began insisting that the hospital release me. I wanted to continue my physical therapy as an outpatient and live in the Bethel Home in Paris. The responsible brethren there came to obtain my release. I wondered who was going to pay the bills. As it turned out, it was the State. I wasn't present at the discussions, but I learned that French socialized medicine covered the hospital costs. Again, "Satan's people" (i.e., the world) had come to the rescue! For the next six months I stayed at the Bethel Home, where there were also offices and a small factory. The Home was situated in Boulogne-Billancourt, a Paris suburb. Once or twice a week, I went to the hospital to use the swimming pool, and a therapist came regularly to my room in headquarters to help me with my exercises.

After a while, I was given some work to occupy me in my room. This helped me to pass the time and feel that I was doing something worthwhile. I even began a little bookbindery department and taught a couple of Bethel workers how to repair, sew, and rebind their library books. This project kept me busy until I left. I was able to participate in the ministry with other Bethel members, and I attended meetings in the congregation that met in the building. Learning to express myself before a crowd in French would be useful to me later. Sometimes I was extremely lonely. Even though I enjoyed the daily visits of the translator of the *Awake!* magazine and all the fellowship with the young people there, I was often depressed and in a bad mood. In spite of this, I was fond of everyone there. I never suspected that someday I would return to France under very different circumstances.

I was using one cane now for my daily walks around the neighborhood; I always walked alone. Sometimes, I walked down to the river Seine and watched the men play *La Pétanque* (a French bowling game), or I walked to the metro stop, Marcel Sembat, and back.

The end of April 1970, and the time for me to return to Africa, finally arrived. With the little money I had been able to save during my stay at the hospital and Bethel, I bought a gold chain and a pearl for Monique. It seemed incredible, but I would be getting married in just a couple of days. I was surprised when I cried as I said good-bye to my friends. We were united in one cause: to preach Jehovah's name and to set Babylon's captives free.

CHAPTER 8

A Mother Turns Her Back on Her Children

As the plane descended, taking me back to the Ivory Coast, I was so happy to think that at last my dreams were coming true. I breezed through customs, since Emile, one of Jehovah's Witnesses who worked for the *Sureté Nationale*, saw to it that I got right through. What a crowd at the airport! To hold Monique in my arms again, to see all the welcomers, and to kiss and hug everyone was one of the happiest moments of my life. When we arrived at the missionary home, Monique informed me that we still had some paperwork to complete before we could get married. I was more than a little surprised; I had thought there would be nothing to it. The ceremony was scheduled for the next Saturday, May 9, and I wondered if it would be possible to get everything in order in time!

A visit to city hall and the marriage bureau gave us some hope. We discovered that we needed only a recent copy of our birth certificates. In French this is called *un extrait*, and it is used for all important events. We went to the American embassy and explained our predicament. The consul, appreciating our dilemma, offered to make a photocopy of my original birth certificate and attach a red ribbon and a stamp. It passed inspection. Monique, however, had to send a telegram to Canada to obtain her copy, and we simply would have to wait for it to arrive.

Friday afternoon, the day before our wedding, Monique's birth certificate still hadn't arrived. The man in charge of marriages in Abidjan said we wouldn't be able to get married without it. We protested, explaining that a lot of people would be coming from Bouaké and other places for the event and that they would be very angry if they made a trip for nothing. Finally, he said: "Okay, you can get married tomorrow; but, as soon as your *extrait de naissance* arrives, you bring it here, and I'll put it into the file." What a relief. As it turned out, the paper arrived on the Monday after the wedding.

For our honeymoon, I had made reservations at a hotel on the beach. The decor was magnificent. In the balmy evenings, we ate outdoors under conical grass huts that were completely open on the sides. After about three days at this romantic place, we began to recognize what it was costing us, a couple of missionaries. Was it necessary, we asked ourselves. Besides, we wanted to visit with the other missionaries and do things together. We packed our bags and surprised everyone at the Adjamé home by showing up a week early. When the honeymoon was over, we learned that we were receiving new assignments.

I went to Bouaké to get my things, since we were being assigned to the capital; I was to replace the congregation servant (a missionary) in Treichville, because he and his wife were expecting a baby. He was leaving the missionary service because of his wife's pregnancy. I had to learn how to carry out the various duties he had been performing. I would now be in charge of the literature depot, the importation of literature and missionary belongings, and the translation of the Kingdom Ministry.

There were fourteen missionaries living in the Treichville home over the Kingdom Hall. We held our weekly study of *The Watchtower*, just as we had done in Bethel. The literature storeroom was downstairs, and we had all the literature for the Ivory Coast and Upper Volta. As the orders for literature came in, I filled them and sent them out. Another responsibility I received was helping in the preparation of the na-

tional convention programs. I was named convention servant.
This meant assigning different parts, discourses, and roles in
sketches or dramas to the brothers and sisters and then over-
seeing their rehearsals. When the Society's vice president,
Fred W. Franz, came to the Ivory Coast for the convention, I
translated his speech.

The time (April–May) arrived to celebrate the Memorial,
which is the commemoration of the death of Jesus. This is
the only holiday or festival that Jehovah's Witnesses consider
important. They carefully check the calendar and schedule
their celebration according to the spring equinox. We
searched our *Watchtower* magazines for the proper recipe and
began preparing the bread (like Jewish matzo) from whole
wheat flour. Then we carefully chose a red wine with no
additives. We invited all our Bible students and everyone we
knew to this most sacred day of the year. As congregation
overseer, I gave the sermon and presided over the meeting.
The ushers had been instructed to take note of those who
drank the wine and ate the bread, because we wanted to
record the number of persons who partook of the meal.
Those who did would signify by their actions that they were
part of the remnant of the 144,000, therefore destined to life
in heaven after their death. In Brooklyn, I had seen a number
of people eat the bread and drink the wine. But here in
Treichville, after the wine and the bread had been passed to
everyone, not a single person drank or ate. It seems like a
farce to me now, to pass something around knowing no one
can partake. Afterward, we filled out the special report card
and sent it to our branch headquarters in Ghana. They would
note the statistics and then forward them to Bethel headquarters in New York.

When the work was banned in Gabon and in the Malagasy Republic (Madagascar), the Malagasy branch servant
and his wife were assigned to Treichville. I felt a little awk-
ward directing things with a former branch servant sitting at

the table. During a zone visit (an inspection by a member of the Brooklyn headquarters) by Brother Don Adams of the president's office, Monique and I learned we were being sent to Gagnoa to begin a new work. Two German sisters, one from my own Gilead class and a new arrival, were assigned to work with us.

I went to Gagnoa to look for a villa to rent and found one just outside of town. As usual, it would serve as our home and meeting place. Gagnoa is in the midst of the Beté tribe, which is known for its aggressiveness (so I was told). In fact, this was the tribe that had caused the Witnesses trouble in the past, resulting in their being banned. I couldn't help feeling a little apprehensive.

We divided up the territory, and Monique and I took the area closest to the missionary home so that I wouldn't have too far to walk. I also chose a section in the middle of Gagnoa that had a lot of boutiques. This would be good for literature placements, because it was practically virgin territory. We began our work as usual, inviting people to meetings in our home and starting Bible studies. Things seemed to be going along pretty well. We didn't have any conflicts in the home, and the Germans were good workers. A couple of my students were showing promise, meaning they were likely to get baptized.

Then things got a little complicated. Monique had been losing weight and hadn't been feeling well in the morning. We decided she needed to see a doctor to find out what was wrong. It didn't occur to me that she could be pregnant. We were shocked to discover that she was. We weren't overjoyed at the news; we were stunned. We felt we had a catastrophe on our hands. Our desire all along had been to avoid having children in order to serve Jehovah full time. Now, with a baby on the way, we no longer could be missionaries. We told our close friends in Adjamé about our "problem". They counseled us not to be in any hurry, to wait and see. It would be rash to make plans to leave the home before we were absolutely sure that her pregnancy was progressing well. After all, she could lose the baby.

Brother Knorr was in Abidjan making a zone visit. It was strange that we hadn't been invited to meet with him. I was a little put out about it, but I let it be known that I was coming to talk with him. Before his visit, I had been making plans to leave the missionary home. I was looking for work, because I wanted to stay in the Ivory Coast and continue spreading the good news as a local publisher. Since I hadn't yet found any employment, I needed a little money for rent until I could begin receiving a paycheck. A couple of JWs offered to lend me the money, but I didn't want to accept anything from my African brothers. I knew they didn't have a lot. I thought perhaps Knorr, the president of our organization, our spiritual mother, would help us.

When I arrived, I was warned that Knorr was upset to find that we were still living in the missionary home. He saw that Monique's hours were low—in other words, we were not productive. This overshadowed our discussion. I didn't get much of his time, and he didn't even invite me to sit down; we stood facing each other. I explained the situation and asked for a two-hundred dollar loan to help us move out of the home. He said that I should ask my parents for the money. I replied: "Brother Knorr, for fourteen years I have served the organization full time, despite my parents' opposition. I don't think it would be appropriate to ask them for help now that we are in a fix." "Well," Knorr said, "they're still your parents, aren't they?" "Yes," I replied, "but the Society teaches us that she is our mother, and so I'm asking my spiritual mother to help us out, not my physical mother, who is in the world and has no interest in the truth." But Brother Knorr insisted that it was my parents' place to help us; we were not the Society's problem. We were the ones who had made a baby, when it is the Society's policy that missionaries must be single persons or couples without children. It boiled down to this: one is required to give his all to the work; productivity would be reduced if couples had children.

I made the trip back to Gagnoa convinced that the Society wouldn't back us if we remained to serve them. If something happened to me there, we couldn't expect any help. If this was their attitude, I thought, the best thing would be to return to Quebec or California. Disenchanted, I was beginning to realize the consequences of having given them everything. I explained to Monique that, when I was in Bethel, I had heard rumors that some who needed an operation or had health problems had been asked to leave until they had gotten things taken care of outside (meaning at family or state expense). Now we too were seeing the other side of the lessons on "brotherly love".

A little later on I wrote the Society requesting a letter of recommendation, because I would be seeking employment, informing them that we were now ready to be sent back home. In reply, I received a big shock. They refused to pay for the trip home. My letter guaranteeing repatriation wasn't worth the paper it was written on. I began to protest to the responsible people in Abidjan, threatening that I would picket outside the *Sureté Nationale*. I would let everyone know that JWs wouldn't pay for their missionaries' plane ticket home. (This was simply a threat, not something I expected I would ever do.) Finally the branch received a letter saying the Society would advance us the money for a ticket to New York City. But we didn't want to go there. We would be stepping off a plane with nowhere to go, with no money. So I refused. Finally, they agreed to pay for a ticket to Montreal.

In March 1972, I had absolutely no idea what we were going to do, how we would live. We wanted to continue to be useful to Jehovah in some manner. After spending a week in France with friends we had met in the Ivory Coast, we continued on to Quebec. My father was born in Canada, and it was Monique's home. Also, if the baby were born there, the delivery costs would be covered by Canadian socialized medicine. Monique's father had been a Witness but had not stayed with it after the death of her mother. He chided us continually about the Witnesses and their attitudes, but we dutifully defended the organization.

Some of Monique's friends and JW relatives held a party for us, and we received about two hundred dollars in gifts to help us get started. We didn't go to many meetings while there, so we had little formal contact with the Witnesses. After so many years of meetings, witnessing, and field work, I was somewhat surprised how welcome the change was to me. It was a much-needed rest. Monique's sister and her husband were not Jehovah's Witnesses, so we rather felt as if we were on vacation.

I went to the Canadian immigration office and filled out an application to work in the country. Then my parents called and asked about our plans. During the conversation, Mom told us that if we wanted to come to California and have the baby there, they would pay for the plane fare. She also offered to let us stay with them until we could get on our feet. I said I would think about it. In the meantime, I went to follow up on a lead for a job. We were at the early part of March, and the snowbanks were still quite high. Looking out the bus window, I saw a woman take a hard fall on the icy sidewalk. This made me realize that working in Montreal during the winters with a weak leg (from the polio) could be rather risky for me. California was looking better every minute. After a short discussion with Monique, we called my parents and asked them to forward the money; our baby would be an American after all.

Our arrival in sunny Los Angeles was an unforgettable experience, especially for a Californian who had been away for so many years. Streets lined with palm trees and back yards with swimming pools were clearly visible as the plane began its approach. My parents welcomed us with open arms, taking us into their home, loaning us their car, feeding us, and helping us out in every way. They had opposed the truth and rejected God's organization, yet they were family, full of love and doing what our spiritual mother had refused to do. The only money we had after all these years was what remained from the sale in the Ivory Coast of my library of JW books, a refrigerator, and a tape recorder and the money left over from what we had received in Canada. Since I felt I owed the Society for the return fare from Africa, I immediately sent them one hundred dollars toward the bill. That left me with less than one hundred dollars, a pregnant wife, and no job.

We immediately began fellowshipping with the Venice-Ocean Park congregation of Jehovah's Witnesses. This group meets in the Hall that I helped build when I was seventeen years old. It was good to see old friends from my youth. I couldn't help noticing that they were quite comfortable: spouses, children, good jobs, and nice homes. Apparently, not everyone had been making the best use of "the short time remaining before Armageddon". I was glad to see a high-school buddy who had divorced his wife (my old sweetheart) and had come back to the area. He had become a JW and had married a woman (a divorcée) who had studied the Bible with him. Jehovah's Witnesses allow second marriages, and this has no doubt attracted many Catholics to them. Ruth was ill with heart trouble, and when I saw her last she was bedridden.

I began looking for work, and, after filling out a few applications, I realized that finding a job might not be easy. I had only a high school diploma, and most of my work experience was with the Witnesses. What *marketable* experience did I have? Talking and arguing with people was one, but who needed it? Mom counseled me to go to the welfare bureau and get some help (especially because of the coming birth).

Who knew how long I might be without any income? She said that there were so many unworthy people on welfare; why shouldn't we take advantage of it? She added, "That's what we pay taxes for, Kenny." Even though I felt ashamed, I did as she wished. I was really surprised when I got immediate help. Free hospitalization was the greatest need at the moment.

One day, I got a call from a stranger who had heard that I was looking for work. He was employed by the New York Life Insurance Company and said that they might have a job for me. I went to their office, filled out the application, and took a couple of tests. I didn't have to wait very long for the news that I was accepted. I entered their training school to learn the business. It seemed a job had found me, a job for which I was well suited. I would have lots of opportunity to try to convince people that our plan was the best. Hadn't I been doing just that for most of my life? Little did I suspect where this would lead me.

The instructor for our class was an interesting fellow. He took me to lunch several times, and we got to know each other better. I told him a little about my experience with Jehovah's Witnesses, and he told me that he had been an evangelical missionary in South America. He was a good witness to his religion. It might be wise, I thought, not to order any wine in his company; it might have a negative effect on my witnessing to him later on. He never pushed his ideas on me, but he did give me a little booklet called *The Four Spiritual Laws*[1] and asked me to read it when I had time. He said it was a Gospel booklet. I assured him (smugly) that I would look it over.

When I read it through, I saw it had a drawing of a cross on one of its pages. As I examined it, I felt that it was very simple, too simple for me. It explained that salvation didn't

[1] San Bernardino, Calif.: Campus Crusade for Christ, n.d.

come through personal effort: the reader was just to *believe in Jesus*, and he would be saved. Where had I heard that before? Of course, I knew that one had to put forth a lot of effort to merit Jehovah's favor. So I just tossed his booklet into the trash. But I tore it up first, so nobody else would waste his time reading it. I soon forgot all about it and concentrated on my training program.

Monique was now eighteen days past her due date for delivery. I thought the baby would never come. Finally, one night she woke me and said she was having contractions. We got into the car and sped to the hospital. As we filled out the necessary entrance forms, we made it known once again that we were Jehovah's Witnesses and would not accept any treatments or products that contained blood, especially blood transfusions.

As I waited in the room with Monique, who was having difficulties—she wasn't dilating—the hospital gave me more forms to sign, discharging them of any responsibility. As time passed, I could see the doctor and the interns were worried. They told me to stay in the room with Monique and watch her while they went to their office to talk. They began to talk about doing a cesarean section, and, if they did that, she was going to need blood. Would I sign these papers, they asked again. No, I said, we cannot have any transfusions, even if it means she might die. A faithful JW, I explained to the doctor why we didn't accept blood transfusions. As I watched the machine that monitored the baby's heartbeat, I noted that it was getting a little weaker, and I became very worried for both Monique and the baby. The pressure was tremendous.

While I waited at times outside the room, I prayed to Jehovah, telling him I would do better, work harder in the service, be a servant in the congregation if the brothers wanted, if only he would let Monique live. After all we had been through together, I couldn't imagine losing her. Finally, without any cesarean, Monique delivered the baby. When I saw our son for the first time, through the nursery window, I thought: "Maybe there is a mistake. Is he mine?" There he was, squinty eyes, yellow from a case of jaundice, and wearing a sling over his shoulder because he had a broken collarbone. The little bit of hair he had was red! Nobody in my family had red hair. But he had his name tag on his wrist and they assured me he was our baby. I felt so relieved: we had our baby, Monique was fine, and we could look forward to raising this little treasure to become Jehovah's servant. We gave him all the Bible names we could string together: Jean-Philippe Michel.

PART THREE

Born Again

I say to you, he who hears my word and believes him who sent me, has eternal life; he does not come into judgment, but has passed from death to life. Truly, truly, I say to you, the hour is coming, and now is, when the dead will hear the voice of the Son of God, and those who hear will live.

—JOHN 5:24–25

CHAPTER 9

The Seeds of Doubt

After the baby's birth, we stayed a while longer with my parents. When a Witness couple went to New York to visit their daughter, they invited us to house-sit for them. They also wanted us to open the house for the Tuesday evening book study that met in their home. Naturally, we attended these meetings, but, unintentionally, I began analyzing the conductor's attitudes, his performance. Remember, I was used to leading meetings; now I had a chance to sit back, listen, and analyze. I got the impression that he was smug and judgmental of those who were not JWs. For the first time this attitude grated on me. We were studying material based upon the Old Testament Book of Ezekiel, and everybody trusted the Society's interpretations as the final word. I pondered the fact that the Society had recently adjusted some of their ideas about the Book of Daniel. This made me remember an experience I had had when I was pioneering in Maine.

One afternoon I had explained to a woman that the "higher powers" mentioned in Romans 13 were not governments but Jehovah and Jesus.[1] When I arrived home, the latest *Watchtower*[2] was in the mailbox. It explained that these powers were not Jehovah and Jesus, but governments! The "truth" had just changed. Any JW admits that the Society talks about new light and better understanding because of changes (adjustments) in their understanding of things. We

[1] *Let God Be True*, rev. ed. (Brooklyn: WTBTS, 1952), p. 248.

[2] *The Watchtower*, November 1, 1962. The NWT renders "higher powers" as "superior authorities".

had just come full circle on "elders", which were being installed in the congregations. Once upon a time, the position and title of "elders" had been eliminated as being unbiblical. The Society argues that such changes in teaching are merely due to the light of understanding growing brighter and brighter as time goes on. They base their idea on Proverbs 4:18: "But the path of the righteous is like the light of dawn, which shines brighter and brighter until full day." For the first time since I had joined the JWs, I was beginning to wonder if this were true in their case.

At the Kingdom Hall, several times when our book study conductor came over to greet me, he said: "Kenny, I don't understand how you can justify selling insurance. You know these people aren't going to be around to collect on their policies. All these promises about the money they are going to save in insurance—you know that they're not going to see age sixty-five with Armageddon so close." His smug assurance and the question bothered me, and I was offended by his question, since I was making a living, and he seemed to be questioning my integrity. Even if his idea had merit, it seemed he should have been happy I had a job and we weren't a burden to anyone. Was he expressing something that others were saying behind my back? I didn't know, but his remarks did push me to think about the wisdom of basing our future on the Society's predictions.

How practical should we be; how much foresight should we exercise? It was now the summer of 1972, and Armageddon was supposed to come around October 1975. But what if it didn't, I thought, and if I pioneered until age sixty-five without ever paying social security. I couldn't picture the Witnesses saying, "Don't worry. We were wrong, and so we will take care of you in your old age." Experience had made me a little wiser. My intuition told me that a responsible person should plan for his old age, despite the fact that he might never live to see it. I found myself looking for some reasoning that would convince a JW to plan ahead, buy insurance, think of death as a possibility, in the eventuality that Armageddon didn't come as soon as expected.

I felt as if I were being pressured on every side: on the job, where I had to prospect for customers, convince, sell, and provide a secure situation for people; by the JWs, with whom I had to canvas, convince, sell, make disciples, and get people into the organization, the ark of safety. I began to feel a great desire for spirituality developing within me. Something was missing, something was lacking, and it certainly wasn't the first time in my life that I had taken note of it. When we attended JW meetings, I noticed they seemed so similar to the training meetings we had in the insurance business: learning how to approach people, overcome objections, and sell the product. Both parties wanted me to be successful and a performer, to put in more hours, and to produce—for them.

I looked for the needed comfort in my meetings, but I didn't feel any better on the way out than I had before I entered the building. I wanted to feel encouraged and uplifted, but the meetings actually had the opposite effect on me. I often left feeling that I needed to work harder, to spend more hours witnessing. After so many years of doing my utmost, I now felt I wasn't performing according to the Society's expectations. Yet, I also wanted to spend more time with my family. I loved Monique and the baby so much. We now had our own apartment, and it was the first time we had lived alone since our marriage. We were poor; the lamp was set on a cardboard box, and the furniture was secondhand, but it was home! So, for the first time since I had become a JW, I began to feel discouragement building up. Reflecting on this, I thought, "I know what I need: I need some spiritual edification. I need to read something up-building. I'll begin reading through the Bible." Since my time was limited, I decided to spend less time preparing meetings and reading the

Society's magazines. I thought to myself, I'll go directly to the source of our literature, the Bible—certainly, I have the necessary training to read it correctly.[3]

Because I was so familiar with the NWT, I decided to use another translation. Taking the phone book, I searched for the closest Bible bookstore. I found an evangelical bookstore located in Culver City, not far from the house. So I went there and looked at several Bibles. I ended up choosing an expensive edition of the *New English Bible*, because it was very fluid in style and had a full-grain leather cover and gilded edges. Responding to a question from the saleslady, I mentioned that I was a minister. She asked, "What denomination?" I replied, "Jehovah's Witnesses." She said, "Oh", her voice dropping off a little, clearly disappointed.

I took my Bible home and prayerfully asked Jehovah to help me decide where to begin reading. I felt strongly the need for something that would build me up. In my heart I was experiencing such a strong thirst for God, for his Word. Dwelling on this, I thought: "No need to start with Genesis, I need something more spiritual. I'll begin with the New Testament and leave the Old Testament for later. I considered reading the epistle either to the Hebrews or to the Romans; these were *meaty* books, books that required lots of thought. I decided on Romans and began looking for the first chapter.

---

[3] That Bible reading can be very dangerous for a JW was something I didn't know then. Long ago, C. T. Russell wrote: "If he then lays them [*Studies in the Scriptures*] aside and ignores them and goes to the Bible alone, though he has understood his Bible for ten years, our experience shows that within two years he goes into darkness. On the other hand, if he had merely read the *Studies in the Scriptures* with their references, and had not read a page of the Bible, as such, he would be in the light at the end of the two years, because he would have the light of Scriptures." Statement found in Raymond F. Franz, *In Search of Christian Freedom* (Atlanta: Commentary Press, 1991), p. 30 (*Watch Tower*, September 15, 1910, reprints p. 4685); also quoted by David A. Reed, editor, in *Index of Watch Tower Errors, 1879 to 1989* (Grand Rapids: Baker Book House, 1990), p. 64.

Turning the pages, I found myself looking at the eighth chapter, and for some reason I began reading the first couple of lines:

> The conclusion of the matter is this: there is no condemnation for those who are united with Christ Jesus, because in Christ Jesus the life-giving law of the Spirit has set you free from the law of sin and death.

Similar to the NWT, which has "in union with Christ Jesus", the NEB said "united with Christ Jesus". As I meditated upon this passage, it struck me as a coincidence that I, who was feeling some condemnation and thought I should be working harder, would open the Bible and land on such a verse! I considered myself to be in union with Christ Jesus, yet I still felt some condemnation. Curious, I read on, seeking an explanation. I came to verse nine:

> But that is not how you live. You are on the spiritual level, if only God's Spirit dwells within you; and if a man does not possess the Spirit of Christ, he is no Christian.

This didn't give me any relief whatsoever. What does it mean to have, or not to have, the Spirit of Christ? Thinking about it, my JW-trained mind responded: "Oh, this must mean having the same *mental attitude* that Christ had about things." (I had been instructed that there were many different ways to understand *spirit* in the Bible.[4]) That seemed to make sense, until I considered that the passage had previously mentioned the Spirit of God; that could mean only God's active force (the JW way of referring to the Holy Spirit, who they think is an invisible *power*, similar to electricity). So I asked myself, "How can we go from the Holy Spirit to a mental attitude within the same verse? How can we be sure it is referring to Christ's mental attitude here? It seemed to me that, in verse

[4] Seven actually: see *Make Sure of All Things* (Brooklyn: WTBTS, 1953), under *Spirit*.

nine, "God's Spirit" and the "Spirit of Christ" could be referring to the same thing (or person).

As I read on, I came to verse 14: "For all who are moved
by the Spirit of God are sons of God" (NEB). Two things
came to mind: was I, or was I not, "led by" [NWT] the Spirit
of God? Well, not directly, because all of a sudden I understood that this chapter was not addressed to me. Paul was
writing to the 144,000, because they are the only ones God
adopts as his spiritual sons! The 144,000 are the only ones
included in Christ's New Covenant for a heavenly kingdom.

As I meditated upon these things, something the Apostle
Paul wrote in Ephesians came to mind: "There is one body
and one Spirit, just as you were called to the one hope that
belongs to your call, one Lord, one faith, one baptism."[5] Yet I
had been taught that there were two hopes: 144,000 hoped
to go to heaven, and the rest of JWs hoped to live forever on
the earth. Sadly, I realized that very little of the New Testament was written directly for the members of the "great
crowd", of which I was a part.[6] What a shame; I wanted to be
able to read the New Testament as God's Word for all Christians, as God's Word for me. Was it really true that Christians
were divided into two groups: some destined for heaven and
the rest for life on earth? Since this seemed to contradict
what Paul wrote to the Ephesians, I began to question it for
the first time since I had entered the group at age seventeen.

I told Monique that I had decided to make an intensive
and objective study of the Bible, particularly the New Testament. I expected to spend a year on it. I had no desire to
leave the organization; the thought never entered my mind,
but something was nagging at me, pushing me to pursue this

---

[5] Eph 4:4, 5 (RSV).

[6] "Also, it is to the spirit-anointed Christians who will rule in that
kingdom that *most* of the Christian Greek Scriptures is directed, including
the promises of everlasting life". *The Watchtower*, June 15, 1974, p. 376;
emphasis is that of *The Watchtower*.

study. I began reading, searching the Scriptures as the Watchtower Society encouraged people to do. I decided to "prove all things", to hold fast to that which was right. I wanted to be like the Bereans, who received the preaching of Paul "with all eagerness, examining the Scriptures daily to see if these things were so" (Acts 17:11).

Here is where someone will ask: "Hadn't you read the Bible through when you were a Witness? You were convinced of their doctrines then, weren't you?" I heard these questions afterward. The answer is yes, but then I lacked *maturity*, I was young, a follower. Now I was thirty-two years old and had been a Witness for sixteen years. I had been to Bethel and met the leadership. I had become acquainted with the reference books the Society uses. I believed I could research these matters as well as anyone else. I knew from experience that the leadership was not always right, otherwise they would not have made so many "adjustments". As time passed, I began comparing our ministry with my insurance job, and I developed a certain distaste for this kind of religious selling and *enticement*, swaying people to study with us. I knew people didn't know what they were getting into when they permitted us to enter their homes over a period of time. Since I had a long record of preaching behind me, I knew I had nothing to prove; I wondered if I would continue in this type of door-to-door work. I made up my mind I wouldn't do it just to please someone else or to have a good record. I would continue only if I was completely convinced after my studies that what the Society teaches really was the truth after all.

As I continued my Bible reading, I began to entertain some doubt about the possibility of salvation based upon my efforts to be faithful to this organization. Would I always be as good as I am now, I wondered. What assurance did I have that I would always be as faithful to Jehovah as I had been? I was only human; I knew I wasn't perfect. I concluded that if salvation depended on me, on *my* strength and *my* good works, as I had been taught, then I didn't have any real assurance for the future.

The Society instructed us that we first of all had to get through Armageddon, and then we would face a thousand-year period called the Judgment Day. This period would be concluded with a final testing of mankind. Only after the perfected ones passed this test would they, upon the basis of their own merits, be adopted as God's sons and receive eternal life. Furthermore, we would have to stand before God without any help from Christ Jesus.[7] Would I make it? One thousand years is a long time!

My investigation was gradually leading me beyond what I had intended. I knew we were forbidden to read books written by ex-JWs; we were told that to do so would be fellowshipping with apostates. We were not even supposed to think negative thoughts! We were to trust the organization as God's channel for spiritual food. Yet, I knew I had to exercise some independence, otherwise an objective study of the truth wouldn't be possible. I went to the Santa Monica library to consult whatever books I could find on Jehovah's Witnesses. I found one by an ex-circuit servant who had left the organization. Although he didn't offer any real spiritual answers, I had to agree with him that the Society seemed to ask an awful lot of its members and to give little in return (that is, *if* they were wrong about Armageddon and the promised paradise). I decided to read *Thirty Years a Watchtower Slave*,[8] about which I had heard so much during my pioneer days but had always refused to read. Looking for more books, I returned to the evangelical bookstore and spoke

[7] *Life Everlasting—In Freedom of the Sons of God* (Brooklyn: WTBTS, 1966), p. 400; also, *Babylon the Great Has Fallen! God's Kingdom Rules* (Brooklyn: WTBTS, 1963), pp. 644–46.

[8] William J. Schnell, *Thirty Years a Watchtower Slave* (Grand Rapids: Baker Book House, 1958).

with the saleslady. She recommended *The Kingdom of the Cults*, by Dr. Walter Martin.[9] Looking it over, I decided to buy it. The book discussed some other groups that also interested me, and I particularly wanted to read the author's treatment of Jehovah's Witnesses.

Then came another trip to the bookstore, this time to buy a Greek–English lexicon, which I needed to check Dr. Martin's accusations concerning some of the renderings in the JWs' Bible. Was it really "as literal a translation as possible",[10] as the preface claimed? Was their translation of John 8:58—"Before Abraham came into existence, I have been"— "word for word, the exact statement of the original"[11]? Or was the Society guilty of violating its own guidelines by paraphrasing, possibly introducing its own doctrines into the text? Back at the library, I checked what Greek scholar A. T. Robertson had to say on John 8:58. After all, the Witnesses had quoted him in the appendix of their own *Kingdom Interlinear Translation* (KIT). Then I moved on to Philippians 2:6 and other verses that touched upon the deity of the Lord Jesus.

By this time, I had changed companies. I was working for the Travelers Insurance Company in Encino. My neighbor, Dean, was a manager there and had hired me. I now had a salary instead of straight commissions. Dean and Sara were Baptists and a wonderful couple. I used to watch them go to church faithfully each Sunday. All the while I was reading *The Kingdom of the Cults*. Reflecting over much of what Dr. Martin said, my reaction was: "I can answer all that." Still, he

[9] Walter R. Martin, *The Kingdom of the Cults*, rev. ed. (Oakland, N.J.: Bethany Fellowship, 1968).

[10] *The Kingdom Interlinear Translation of the Greek Scriptures* (Brooklyn: WTBTS, 1969), p. 10; abbreviated hereafter as KIT. This New Testament contains the Greek text with the word-for-word translation below each Greek word and then the current NWT text in the parallel column.

[11] Ibid.

scored several points, and I wanted to spend more time on them. One day, Dean and Ken (another manager and Baptist) invited me out to lunch. Swell, I thought, free lunch and with the boss, too. "Okay, I'll go", I replied. "Great," they said, "but we need to tell you something." They explained that they would be going to a restaurant in Van Nuys, where every Thursday a group of men ate together. After the meal, someone gave a testimony about Jesus Christ, and they thought that the speaker for this week might interest me. Hearing this, I hesitated. I wouldn't enter anyone's church, as that would be possible grounds for excommunication; also, what would I hear of interest? But I supposed I could tolerate the meeting if it furnished me with some new contacts that could lead to more sales. So I agreed to go, not realizing how important this meeting would be for my life.

We found the other men in the back of the restaurant, eating and talking together. I was introduced to those facing us on the other side of the table. I was hoping that Dean wouldn't tell them that I was one of Jehovah's Witnesses. I felt like an undercover agent, an infiltrator, surrounded by these so-called Christians. After the meal, someone stood and introduced the speaker. He got to his feet with difficulty. I saw he had a pair of crutches. He began recounting his wartime experiences and how he had been shot down during War World II. He had been left a cripple, and it was a miracle that he could walk. But, he said, the greatest miracle was that he had met Jesus, who had saved him. He told us that if any of us had not yet asked Jesus to come into his life, now was the time to do it. Then he asked us to bow our heads, and he said what is called "the sinner's prayer". "Dear Father, I know that I am a sinner and need your forgiveness. I believe that Christ died for my sin. I am willing to turn from my sins. I now invite Jesus Christ to come into my heart and life as my personal Savior. I am willing, by God's grace, to follow and obey Christ as the Lord of my life."[12]

When he began, I bowed my head, but I thought, "I'm not going to pray any prayers. I can't pray with these guys. We don't worship the same God. My God is Jehovah." We were invited to take home with us the little blue booklet "Do You Know the Steps to Peace with God?" that was beside each plate. Thirty years later, I still have it. Strange, it was almost exactly the same as the booklet I had thrown into the trash can at the New York Life Insurance office. When I got home, I tore out a page containing a quotation from Ephesians 2:8–9. I liked what it said about being saved by grace and not by works. I taped the page to the closet door so that in the morning I could read it as I dressed. I wondered how this verse squared with James 2:26, which says that "faith without works is dead." I didn't know how to harmonize the two, but for the moment I wasn't trying to solve a puzzle. I just felt that Paul's message in Ephesians was very important to me.

I kept on studying. I was so hungry for Christ that I was reading a huge book on the life of Jesus by a converted Jew named Edersheim.[13] I decided to read again the chapter on Jehovah's Witnesses in Walter Martin's book. As I read, I gave particular attention to his quotation from *Thayer's Greek–English Lexicon*[14] on Philippians 2:6. Since it was now in my library, I turned to *Thayer's Lexicon* and the entry for the Greek word *morphe* (Phil 2:6).

[12] Taken from the booklet found at each table setting, "Do You Know the Steps to Peace with God?" (Glen Ellyn, Ill.: Christian Business Men's Committee International, n.d.).

[13] Alfred Edersheim, *The Life and Times of Jesus the Messiah*, rev. ed. (Grand Rapids: Eerdmans, 1953).

[14] Joseph Henry Thayer, ed. and trans., *A Greek–English Lexicon of the New Testament Being Grimm's Wilke's Clavis Novi Testamenti*, 4th ed. (Edinburgh: T. & T. Clark, 1901). This has been reprinted by Zondervan Publishing House.

> *Who, although* (formerly when he was *logos asarkos*) *he bore the form* (in which he appeared to the inhabitants of heaven) *of God* (the sovereign, opp. to *morph. doulou*), *yet did not think that this equality with God was to be eagerly clung to* or *retained.* [15]

It wasn't difficult to see that this explanation could be used to substantiate the Church's teaching on the Trinity. That would explain why saints like Jerome and Augustine, and even the Protestant reformers, believed in the Trinity. How could the Witnesses claim that their version of the Bible was more accurate than others, since they were a relatively recent and small organization when they issued their New Testament in 1950. Surely those who lived closer to the time of Christ were more familiar with the biblical languages than the Watchtower leaders in Brooklyn.

Then I noticed another verse quoted by Martin, 1 Corinthians 12:3: "Therefore I want you to understand that no one speaking by the Spirit of God ever says 'Jesus be cursed!' and no one can say 'Jesus is Lord' except by the Holy Spirit." I opened my Bible to this verse and thought about what it meant to me, a Jehovah's Witness, or to a Jew in Paul's time, or to my Jewish neighbor across the hall. Was Jesus one of many gods and lords, such as Paul mentioned in 1 Corinthians 8:5? It was becoming evident to me that I had placed another god alongside the Almighty God. I thought about how difficult it had been for the Jews to receive Jesus as the Messiah. Hadn't they accused him of blasphemy, of making himself *equal* to God? [16] I had always thought I was a mono-theist, now I could see that I wasn't; I had two gods! I had a big God, Jehovah, and a second god, Jesus! Isaiah says: "Is there a God beside me? Yea, there is no God; I know not any" (Is 44:6–8; KJV). Then I remembered those Old Testament passages that spoke of God as Jehovah yet seemingly

[15] Ibid., p. 418.
[16] See Mk 14:62–64; Jn 5:18; 10:30–33.

found their fulfillment in Jesus.[17] I could see where this line of reasoning was taking me, yet I also could see that it would indeed take the Holy Spirit's help for me to believe that Jesus is Jehovah.

Then it struck me like a bolt of lightning. Of course it would take the Holy Spirit for me to believe such a thing! Neither I nor any one else could believe in Jesus and trust him for salvation without the gift of faith given by the Holy Spirit.[18] It was as if I had been struggling for a long time over some mathematical problem, and all of a sudden I saw the solution, one so simple that I wondered why I hadn't seen it sooner. Physically, it felt as if a light had turned on in my head, and goose bumps ran over me.

I leaped out of my chair and almost ran to the kitchen to share my discovery with Monique: "Look at this", I exclaimed. "I think I've discovered something." When she heard it, she didn't show the slightest interest. She was nervous, worried about where these investigations were leading me. She knew full well what would happen to anyone who didn't adhere strictly to the Society's teachings. It could even cause problems in our marriage. Disappointed, I returned to my chair and to my thoughts. I decided I would continue testing my ideas. I wouldn't let emotions carry me away, either. Maybe Jesus was Jehovah; I could almost admit it now, but I must make sure. Then what about the Trinity, hell, the soul, Armageddon, and other things, such as that God accepts Jehovah's Witnesses as his people?

One morning at the office, Ken approached me at my desk. "Hi, how're you doing?", he asked. He sat down and lost no time getting to the point. He wanted to witness to me! He asked me if I was sure of going to heaven when I died. I said no, I was planning to live forever on earth. He

---

[17] For example, Joel 2:28–32, fulfilled in Acts 2:16–38 and Rom 10:1–17.

[18] Eph 2:8–9 and Jn 6:37, 44.

stressed that I could go to heaven, but I would have to know Jesus Christ personally as my Savior. I quickly saw that we weren't going to get anywhere in this discussion because he didn't seem to know very much about JWs (at least, that's what I thought). So I said: "If you are really serious about discussing these things, the best thing to do is to make an appointment with your minister for us all to get together some Saturday afternoon. Then you can watch." (I thought I would probably be able to show the two of them a thing or two.) Then Ken mentioned a book he was reading and wanted to recommend to me. He said the title was *The Kingdom of the Cults*. "Hey, I'm reading the same book. That's really a coincidence", I told him. We talked a little more, and that was it.

In the meantime, I found a book on the Trinity[19] by Edward Bickersteth and began studying it carefully. I continued to attend Christian Business Men's meetings from time to time, listening and evaluating the testimonies of the men. A little later on, I accepted an invitation to visit Dean's church when they were having some evangelistic services. I liked what I heard and saw. Next, we made an appointment for our families to meet with Ken and his wife for the Sunday morning services at Van Nuys First Baptist Church, where Dr. Harold Fickett, Jr., was pastor. This was truly a beautiful church. We sat up in the balcony, and, as the service was in progress, I was thinking: "They're really giving me the works, taking me to such a big, beautiful church." During his sermon, the pastor had something to say about Jehovah's Witnesses. I wondered whether they had told him I would be present. I heard the "altar call" at the end of the service and watched the people praying with heads bowed. I was looking

[19] Edward Henry Bickersteth, *The Trinity, Scripture Testimony to the One Eternal Godhead of the Father, and of the Son, and of the Holy Spirit* [originally, *The Rock of Ages, or Three Persons but One God*] (Grand Rapids: Kregel Publications, 1957).

The First Baptist Church in Van Nuys, California

around, marveling at their devotion, their sincerity. I appreciated the simple call to come to Jesus, not to join some organization, be it a church or some other kind. I would think about it, I thought. I wasn't going to let emotions take over.

One afternoon, I finally decided to go visit a pastor at First Baptist Church in Van Nuys. Perhaps I could ask him some of my toughest questions. I was sincere; I wanted help. I wanted him to explain the Old Testament passages on the soul and hell. The question of Jesus' identity no longer bothered me as much. Still, I was very unsure of myself. It seemed incredible that the Watch Tower Society could be wrong, I had trusted it so completely. When I showed up at the church office and requested to see the pastor, the receptionist sent me to the pastoral care offices, which were located in another building. I took the elevator and found the office. I told the secretary there that I was a Jehovah's Witness, but that I was open. I wanted to talk to one of the pastors. I remember well the one who stepped out of his office to speak with me. His name was Ed Kriz; he was in charge of pastoral care. When he heard what I wanted, he said, "Wait a minute, I am not qualified on that; I have had some bad experiences with JWs. But I do know of a man who is an expert on the topic. In fact, he gave a conference here in our church not very long ago. I'll give you his address and phone number, and you can go talk with him." As he gave me the information, he added that the man was a professor at Los Angeles Baptist College in Newhall, and, what is more, he had once been a JW himself! I had never spoken with an ex-Jehovah's Witness before; it was forbidden. But I figured I had come this far, I might as well go and see him.

I called Professor Ed Gruss, and we made an appointment to meet in his home. A tall, pleasant man met me at the door. He invited me into the back of the house, where he had a large office with file cabinets and rows of books. I could see that many of his books were JW publications. He had entire sets of *Studies in the Scriptures*, written by C. T. Russell, the founder and first president of Zion's Watch Tower and Tract Society, as it was first called. I felt a little uneasy as we began. I confessed that this was the first time I had knowingly spoken with a former Jehovah's Witness. He smiled and asked me to relate my story in detail. As I talked, he interrupted me from time to time to ask a question. The time sped by, and, before I realized it, we had spent a couple of hours together.

Gruss was professor of history and apologetics. He had written his master's thesis on Jehovah's Witnesses, and it had been published under the title *Apostles of Denial*. My copy has the date I received it from him, February 8, 1973, the date of our first meeting. When I left Ed, I was much more openminded than when I had entered. I would read the book, I told him. On the way out, Ed handed me a cassette made by a Baptist minister who also had been a JW.

I did my homework. I read his book, listened to the cassette tape, and prayed. Something in the cassette drew my attention to a matter of which I was aware but had not fully appreciated. We Jehovah's Witnesses were working for our salvation. I knew that. But something struck me when the speaker, the Rev. Ted Dencher, read a quotation from the book *Life Everlasting—In the Freedom of the Sons of God*:

> Jehovah God will justify, declare righteous, *on the basis of their own merit* all perfected humans who have withstood that final, decisive test of mankind. He will adopt and acknowledge them as his sons through Jesus Christ (Rom 8:33).[20]

I clearly understood what this meant, not only for me, but for the precious sacrifice that Jesus gave for us on the Cross. He died to expiate sin. No one, by means of the Law of Moses or anything else, should be able to say: "*I have earned the right* to be a son of God, to receive eternal life." Yet the JWs were teaching just such a heresy. According to them, people were going to become perfect, and afterward they would be tested and adopted as sons of God on the basis of their own merit. I could no longer accept this. There was no doubt in my mind that this was the doctrine of the Antichrist, completely opposed to Christianity, which teaches that God is the one who justifies us.

I now believed that eternal life is "the gift of God" granted through the Savior, Jesus Christ (Jn 4:10; Eph 2:8–9; Rom 6:23); it cannot be earned or merited as the JWs teach. The day had finally arrived . . . In the privacy of my bedroom I got down on my knees and prayed: "Lord, Jesus, I know that you died for my sins. I know that you want to save me from them. A church, a religion, didn't die for me. I don't really believe that I can save myself, that I can be good enough to merit salvation. I'm done following men, churches, or whatever. I will follow you. I want you to save me. I am entrusting you with my life, my salvation, my future. Please save me. If you can't, no one else can do it. I place my life, my entire self, in your hands. Please give me

---

[20] P. 400, emphasis added.

the gift of eternal life." I rose from my knees feeling that a great weight had been lifted from my shoulders. I still didn't know a lot about *right doctrine*; I didn't have all the answers. If I died on the spot, I felt I had done all that I could. I had received and trusted God's Son for my salvation.[21] That day, that very moment, I got back on the road to freedom, peace, and happiness. I had returned to *El Camino Real*.

I made another appointment to see Ed Gruss. This time during our conversation, he asked me what I thought about Jesus Christ and how I thought I would be saved. I told him what had happened since I had last seen him, and I explained my convictions about salvation and new birth (Jn 3:3–5). I'll never forget his words. He said: "I think you are already born again." With great emotion, and tears rolling down my cheeks, I said: "Do you really think so?" Ed then gave me a copy of another book he had written: *Jehovah's Witnesses and Prophetic Speculation*. He autographed it for me on the title page. "To Ken: May God bless and use you for His glory. Ed. Acts 1:8. March 17, 1973."

I left Ed's home and made the drive back to our apartment in Mar Vista. I wanted to begin reading the book right away. This one covered prophetic matters from the Society's origins to the present. The necessary documentation was presented from the Society's own literature and in a very scholarly manner. It demonstrated how the Society's founder, C. T. Russell, and, later, J. R. Rutherford and his successors were guilty of false prophesying. The Society claimed to speak in God's name and used the Bible to support such claims. I was aware of the accusation that the Society had prophesied that the end of the world would come in 1914, but I really didn't know much about it, in spite of my having held positions of responsibility in the organization. Studying the Society's publication *Jehovah's Witnesses in the Divine Pur-*

[21] 1 Jn 4:9, 14.

pose[22] was one thing, but reading the facts, documented and lined up one after the other, dealt a crushing blow to the Society's argumentation (and *pretenses*).

Finally I arrived at page 96 in the book, where, after two pages of direct quotations on prophetic speculation, the author asks: "On the basis of past pronouncements, can the Watch Tower Society be trusted as an accurate source of prophetic understanding?" All remaining doubts and fears were completely banished. I decided to take my stand. I would resign. In the space following the question, I wrote: "No! Ken Guindon, ex-Watchtower missionary." I knew that it would be hard to break with the organization. I feared for our marriage and dreaded fights over the religious education of our son. I had been working on Monique, trying to share what I was learning with her. but I didn't seem to be having any success at all. I planned to wait just a little while longer to give Monique more time, hoping she would come to see the truth. But for me, it was finished. I was free. I would no longer follow such a group. I would follow Jesus, the Lamb of God. I didn't know it then, but I was at the halfway point on what would still be a long road home.

[22] Brooklyn: WTBTS, 1959.

CHAPTER 10

Resigning from the Organization

> And he called to him the multitude with his disciples,
> and said to them, "If any man would come after me, let
> him deny himself and take up his cross and follow
> me. . . . For whoever loses his life for my sake and the
> gospel's will save it. For what does it profit a man, to
> gain the whole world and forfeit his life?
> —MARK 8:34–35

I had accepted Christ as my Savior, but I had not joined a
church. I hadn't become anything more than a Christian. In
my thinking at that point in time, the most important step
was accepting and receiving Jesus as my Lord, God, and Savior. I hadn't become a Baptist or anything else. I certainly had
no desire to return to the Catholic Church. In fact, that was
the farthest thing from my mind. I was still very anti-Catholic
and, in fact, quite skeptical about any church. Physically, out-
wardly—but definitely not inwardly and spiritually—I was
still a member of the Jehovah's Witnesses. But that was soon
going to change.

In January 1973, I turned in my last report of field-service
activity. I began refusing assignments to give talks, pleading
that I didn't have time. I didn't go as frequently to meetings
during the week. It was difficult to give a reasonable explanation. I didn't want to tell anyone about my doubts. When two
close friends tried to encourage me, I couldn't help raising a
few questions during our conversations.

During *The Watchtower* study on Sunday, several times I had the opportunity to point out to Monique things that I knew were wrong. One of these was concerning the requirement for the Son of God to preach faithfully unto death in order that he might obtain eternal life. *The Watchtower's* presentation was shocking. Here is the quotation in question:

> He preached good news to the poor, comforted mourners and declared Jehovah's day of vengeance to high and low alike. Jesus worked what was good, was rich in fine works, was most liberal with his time and energy in behalf of others, was ready to share his great knowledge and wisdom with others, and in the end he finally got a firm hold on the real life, everlasting life in the heavens with his Father—John 18:37; 1 Timothy 6:12, 18, 19; Hebrews 5:8. In all of this Jesus also left us a model that we might follow his steps closely.[1]

This quotation should be contrasted with what the Bible really teaches about Jesus in the Gospel of John (1:4, 5:21, 24, 26; 6:35; 11:25). These last references are the ones I wrote down years ago in the margin of the photocopy I kept of this page. It was perfectly clear to me then that the Society was willing to use any argument, no matter how ridiculous, to push the door-to-door work. When they use Christ as a model for the preaching work, it is evident that there is no limit to the extremes to which they are willing to go. To claim that he who is Life "in the end finally got a firm hold on the real life, everlasting life in the heavens", was too much. It made me sick. I elbowed Monique, pointed out the statement, and told her in French that I wanted to leave.

I didn't have much time left in the organization, maybe just a couple more meetings. In the meantime, I found them boring, repetitious, and mechanical, in fact, very similar to brainwashing sessions. The method was totally controlled; no one was allowed to question Society practices or doctrines.

[1] This is an exact quote from *The Watchtower* of January 1, 1973 (p. 20), and it includes supporting proof texts.

Because my back grew tired from sitting so long, I often stood at the back of the hall. Sometimes I went outside to get some fresh air. I prayed fervently, "Oh, God, help us. Send your Spirit into Monique's heart that she might see what you have shown me."

The time came to make a break; I had to follow my conscience, even though the cost might be terrible. One Sunday morning I told Monique that I was not going to the meeting with her that day or ever again. I explained that I had made arrangements to attend a Baptist church with Dean and Sara. I invited her to come with me, but I also offered to drive her to the JW meeting if that was her preference. I then told her I was planning to write my resignation letter that very day. I would respect her decision to remain a member of the organization, I said, but I would not allow our son to be taught JW doctrines. Tears were not absent from our discussion, and I was completely surprised by how it ended. At last Monique said she would skip the meeting and accompany Dean, Sara, and me.

We made the forty-minute drive through the Santa Monica mountains to the San Fernando Valley. Again we sat in the balcony of the church, Monique crying all through the service. After church, we went to Dean's house, where I wrote my resignation letter. As I was signing it, Monique said, "Put my name on that, too."

"What?" I exclaimed. "I can't do that. If you want your name on the letter, you sign it yourself. Besides, you can't leave the Witnesses for me."

"I wouldn't do that; just pass me the paper", she said. I was still uncomfortable with her jumping in like this, so I suggested we discuss it privately first. We went into another room, and I asked Monique if she was sincere. "Do you believe that Jesus is Lord and God?" I asked. "Have you accepted Him into your heart as your personal Savior? Are you trusting Him alone for your salvation?"

"Yes", she said. All the while I was holding her in my arms and crying along with her. Then all of a sudden I felt a little angry that she hadn't told me this before. "When did you do this? How long ago?" I asked. "About two weeks ago", she answered. "It just came to me. It must have been all those people praying for me; otherwise it would never have been possible." I could hardly believe my ears. I was so astonished and at the same time so happy. Our marriage would not be threatened after all, I thought, and our baby would not be in danger of being raised a Jehovah's Witness. I fully realized what a blessing I had received for having made this decision. Praise God!

The next day we went to the post office and sent our letter by certified mail to the Ocean Park Congregation of Jehovah's Witnesses. In the letter, we expressed our appreciation for them but explained that we were withdrawing our membership from the organization because we no longer believed the governing body to be guided by the Holy Spirit. As we anxiously awaited a reply, a JW couple came to visit. We suspected they were probably checking up on us, trying to find out why we were not attending the meetings. We felt obliged to tell them that we had resigned. They undoubtedly reported their conversation to the overseers.

A reply to our letter arrived a couple of weeks later. It was dated April 4, 1973, and signed by the presiding overseer, Guy Young. It said:

> In view of your recent letter and conversations with other brothers in the congregation, we feel that there is evidence of your taking a course of rebellion against the theocratic organization and teaching of false doctrine.
>
> Therefore, the judicial committee of the Ocean Park Congregation of Jehovah's Witnesses would like to meet with both of you on Saturday, April 7, 1973, at 1:00 P.M. at the Kingdom Hall. . . .

For several weeks I had been meeting regularly with Dr. Fickett, the pastor of the Van Nuys First Baptist Church. Someone who heard me give a testimony at the Christian Business Men's luncheon had told him about me. Dr. Fickett had called me at home and asked me to come see him. He wanted me to join his church. After visiting and praying a while on the matter, I decided that this was the church for me. During a conversation, I informed him that the Witnesses had convoked a hearing and asked him if he thought it would serve any purpose to go. He said he thought that it would be a good idea to attend the meeting. He even suggested that I give them a good testimony and tape-record the proceedings.

The day for our meeting with the judicial committee arrived, and I had prepared myself spiritually for it. I took a briefcase packed with a Bible, the KIT, *Thayer's Greek–English Lexicon of the New Testament,* and a tape recorder. When I got there, these good people I loved so much and had known since I was a young man greeted me kindly but seriously. We went into the library and closed the door. The meeting opened with prayer. Then they asked why Monique wasn't there. I told them that she was at my mother's house and that she hadn't wanted to come. She wanted me to tell them they could do what they wanted. (She knew they would disfellowship her.) They still wanted to talk with her personally, so I phoned her. She told me she didn't want to talk with them.

I related my whole story to them. I told them about my discoveries in the Society's older publications, and I explained what I believed about Jesus. I told them I didn't need to knock on doors in order to *gain* eternal life; I had it *now*. I read to them 1 John 5:1 and said I was born again and was now a son of God. Furthermore, I added, Jesus said, "He believes in me has eternal life." I concluded by saying that I was through with the Watchtower Society.

One of them, the youngest member of the three who composed the committee, went to the shelf and took out a bound volume of *The Watchtower*. Evidently he had this prepared, because he knew exactly where the page was. He asked me if I had joined or was going to join a church. I didn't want to make this a battle of denominations, and I knew they would attack any church name I would give them, so I said: "It's not a matter of joining a church in order to be saved. *I am going to Jesus*; he has all I need." This was the truth and the reason I was leaving them. I didn't believe *any* church had all the truth or that one church was the one true church.

When I left the Ivory Coast, the Society had given me a letter stating that I had always been "fully trustworthy and honest", and they gave me their "highest recommendation". Now, I (and Monique) would be considered the lowest of the low, renegades. To any who might bring up my name, the JWs would insist that I was really a bad character. I heard later from some of my new friends that Witnesses told them that I had been disfellowshipped for immorality. They never announce publicly the reason for an excommunication. The congregation must trust the overseers. The congregation members have no say in these matters. Before the entire congregation, the overseer reads the charge: So and so has been "disfellowshipped for conduct unbecoming to a Christian". This leaves it to the imaginations of those present or who may hear about it later to put any interpretation they want on the matter. They can't admit that more *light*, more research, could prove the Society to be in error. They are so sure they have the truth that anyone who disagrees with them has taken Satan's side and must be considered an enemy. Since I had known the truth so well and had served at headquarters, I had to be leaving for some ulterior motive.

One might conclude that they use totalitarian tactics to suppress free speech and investigation. The leaders are the only ones who can write and disseminate literature. The flock must meekly follow, proving they are sheep. The sad thing is they are not following the voice of the true Shepherd, Christ Jesus. When one is disfellowshipped, he is effectively isolated; it is like being exiled to Siberia. He will have no means of communicating with—contaminating—the others. The group considers the apostate to be dead, to be a traitor, to have loved the world more than the truth. He is spoken of as being rebellious, proud, haughty, and every other negative thing imaginable. It is a fact that Jehovah's Witnesses are a government unto themselves. The use of terms like *judicial committee* make this clear. The Witness is to listen, to follow, to work. He must help the organization grow. This growth is considered evidence that God is blessing the organization. To fight them, then, is to fight God himself.

Upon arriving home from work the following week, I discovered two Witness ladies sitting in our living room. They were having a discussion with Monique. When I saw them, I went over to them and bent down to kiss the cheek of Claudia, a longtime friend. I had known her for more than sixteen years. She turned her head away and said, "I can't talk to you; you are disfellowshipped." That was the first time I had heard about it. No one had shown me the courtesy to call me, write me, or tell me in person that I had been disfellowshipped. They had simply read it out in public, and in that instant I became a dead man.

Deciding to leave them alone, I went to my room to study my insurance lessons. The door wasn't completely closed, so I couldn't help overhearing their discussion. The ladies were throwing questions at Monique about what she believed about the soul, hell, Armageddon, and so on. I really felt sorry for her. She was struggling for words to defend herself, to explain why she was leaving the organization. Being the kind of person she is, she had no desire to argue about these things. And she knew she wasn't prepared to do so; she had no formal training in theology or in Christian apologetics.

The only training she had received was from the Watchtower Society. She hadn't read any of the books I had read, and she had never had the time or the desire to do the research I had done. Her break with the Watch Tower Society was certainly due to God's grace.

Finally, I couldn't stand it any longer. I could hear Monique crying. This was my home, and the enemy had entered it and was tormenting my wife, grilling her, and causing her emotional distress. I got up, went to the living room, and said to the women: "You came here behind my back when I wasn't home. You won't speak to someone who can answer your questions. My wife told you that she has left the organization and doesn't want anything more to do with it. That's enough! If you won't talk with me, then leave!" And so they left the house and our lives.

The road we had chosen was not going to be easy; we had no illusions about that. Had not Jesus said: "If any man would come after me, let him deny himself and take up his cross and follow me" (Mk 8:34)? Progress on God's road is difficult at times, because taking up the cross means dying to self. It can be costly in the areas of family, friends, reputation, and financial security. Monique had been a baptized JW for seventeen years, and I for sixteen. For us, the decision to follow Christ cost us all the friends we had known for so many years. Monique's best friend, Marcia, a missionary in the Ivory Coast, wrote to my mother to inquire about us. Having been informed by the Society that we were disfellowshipped, she wanted to know why. She dared not write us directly, of course, so she asked my mother to explain what had happened to us, people who had been so zealous for Jehovah and his organization. She wrote that we were now spiritually dead and had no hope of resurrection in the new world if we didn't repent and come back. When I talked with Monique about this, she said that she really did not feel the hurt. The love of God had so completely filled her heart. She had gained much more than she had lost. And I was impressed by her calm, her inner peace.

Whereas the Jehovah's Witnesses were planning on Armageddon for the fall of 1975, we realized we would have to make other plans. Our only desire was to follow Jesus, to do God's will as we discovered it day by day. We needed to find good literature, do our own research, choose a church, and make new Christian friends with whom we could share our joys and sorrows. As we look back from our present vantage point of time and experience, we can see that we did zigzag a little. We take some comfort in the thought that we are not alone in having searched and struggled to know the truth. Saint Augustine, for example, passed through many twists and turns before finally coming to rest in Christ and in his Church. It would have been better if we had gotten everything 100 percent correct from the beginning. Never to have known the Jehovah's Witnesses, to have remained in God's grace from our childhood, would have been ideal. But that is not the way for many of us. Each person has his own problems to overcome and questions to answer. Each one comes to terms with God and his conscience in a unique way. And sometimes our experiences can be useful when counseling others.

CHAPTER II

A New Baptism and a New Ministry

The day after I met with the judicial committee, Monique and I responded to the altar call at the First Baptist Church of Van Nuys. We were invited to give a short testimony to the audience of about seventeen hundred people. Every Sunday evening, the pastor baptized people in the little pool behind the pulpit. Since Dr. Fickett had already met with me a number of times, we were scheduled for baptism that very evening. It is coincidental that this was exactly sixteen years from the day I had been baptized in a swimming pool in Hollywood, California, by the Jehovah's Witnesses. Dr. Fickett required us to be baptized as a sign that we had received Christ as Savior.

The Baptists reject Catholic baptism as well as baptism by JWs for three important reasons: (1) infants are not able to profess faith in Jesus; (2) the Catholic Church is considered to be apostate, therefore her rites are not recognized; and (3) the mode of baptism as usually practiced in the Catholic Church is pouring, which is completely unacceptable to Baptists, who accept only baptism by immersion. Our baptism by immersion by the Witnesses was rejected because Witnesses deny the Trinity and other important Christian dogmas.

So we entered the Baptist Church by our profession of faith followed by baptism. We were, indeed, very happy to do so, even though we didn't think this was the only true church. We scarcely knew anything about its teachings on prophecy; I was not enthusiastic about what I had read on it

127

(Hal Lindsey's *The Late Great Planet Earth*). Still, we knew we had to meet with other Christians. We didn't want to remain isolated while looking for the perfect group. I believed the Baptists adhered the most closely to the Bible in their teachings. I had eliminated the Lutherans, Methodists, Episcopalians, and Presbyterians because they all baptized babies. The Catholic Church was completely out of the question; everyone I knew agreed that she was the Whore, called Babylon the Great. Strange, the Baptists are so much like the Witnesses on some points of doctrine. They believe that baptism has to be performed by immersion and that the Lord's Supper is a memorial. The ordinances are considered to be only symbols, not sacraments. The Baptists believe that Christ will return at Armageddon to destroy the wicked and rule the world for a thousand years. Only the righteous will enter the millennium. Of course, some of the details are different, but the general outline is the same. So the transition wasn't *that* difficult. Actually, if we had been questioned more closely, they may have wanted us to wait a little longer until we got other doctrines straightened out.

In June, I was asked to present a series of talks on the Jehovah's Witnesses for the adult education class the church held each Sunday evening. This was one of many excellent programs sponsored by Van Nuys First Baptist Church. I was a little nervous about it, because I still didn't have a complete understanding of the soul, hell, and eternal security.[1] I just hadn't had the time to find some qualified person who could spend time answering the many questions I still had. Fortunately, teaching can be one of the best ways to learn. To prepare for the class, I was obliged to do a lot of research. As a result, my grasp of Christian theology greatly improved.

I examined more closely the Witnesses' prophetic statements and their Bible translation. I checked suspicious quo-

[1] Eternal security is a Calvinist doctrine that Baptists sum up in the expression "Once saved, always saved."

tations in their literature and discovered that some were used in a manner contrary to what the author had intended. I researched their history and came to know it better than when I was a Witness. My library of Witness books again grew to the point where I had collected almost all of their publications, including many books long out of print.

All of this investigation strengthened my new faith. One may come free in an instant and have faith in Christ, but no one can spend sixteen years or more with the Jehovah's Witnesses and not be somewhat scarred by the experience. It takes time for a wound to heal and become less painful, less visible. Overcoming the wounds of my past experience with religion and gaining confidence in my new faith also took time. After all, from my adolescence on, I had been very impressed, very convinced, by the Witnesses' teachings. Their writings had seemed so scholarly, so far above me, I naturally was somewhat fearful at leaving them.

I finished the year 1973 growing in the faith and giving testimonies whenever invited to do so. From time to time, I accompanied the church evangelists to various homes. I was amazed to see how God used simple things, a brief testimony, a little encouragement, to build up others. Many times I saw people bow their heads and ask Christ to come into their hearts and lives. I was thrilled. During this time we moved out to the San Fernando Valley to be close to my work in Encino and to our new church.

On the business side, things weren't so rosy. I found my work interesting, but I knew in my heart that it wasn't for me. One day, during a meeting with Dr. Fickett, he asked me to consider joining the church staff with the goal of becoming a minister. The motto of the church was "A Church with a Vision". Harold Fickett, Jr., was a man with a vision and for fourteen years had been leading this church in giving a mighty witness for Christ. This invitation truly corresponded to my heart's secret desire, so I was happy to join the staff in

January 1974. I began my on-the-job training as a visitation minister to those in hospitals and nursing homes. Already I was taking classes in Greek in the little Christian College the church had begun and spending many hours in personal studies.

While working, I continued taking courses at the Christian College, and I also attended classes at Los Angeles Baptist College and later at Talbot Theological Seminary. I was not seeking a degree but simply improving my educational background for the ministry.

My ordination in February 1975 was a great event in my life. Our church had recommended my ordination under the sponsorship of a Baptist body called Conservative Baptists of America. Many of the ministers on our staff were individually affiliated with that group. I was perfectly happy to join with them because they seemed to be pretty much middle of the road, avoiding extremes. I went through two ministerial councils: a preliminary council and the one that finally recommends that the church go ahead with the ordination.

I received much satisfaction from my work at First Baptist. Before long, Dr. Fickett encouraged me to write my testimony. The church distributed one hundred thousand copies of this tract. Then he suggested I write something on the cults, so I began a paper called "The Defense". It did quite well for such a little thing. The church recorded my Sunday evening teaching sessions on the Jehovah's Witnesses. My tapes made up 10 percent of the cassette production that year. Our outreach to Jehovah's Witnesses produced fruit over the years. Some Jehovah's Witnesses converted and were baptized in our church. One woman had been a Witness for twenty-five years. Many people who were studying with them stopped and began associating with our church.

In spite of the growth and success of First Baptist, during the mid 1970s, the church began to crumble under the weight of problems endemic to mainstream Protestantism.

Many Christians seemed to be searching for "more" and moving away from mainstream denominations. The charismatic movement was growing stronger. Stories of miracles, healings, and other wonders were circulating in our church, and many members were sincerely seeking a renewal of God's presence in their lives. Some of my best friends in the church were telling me there was more than simply accepting Christ; one also needed to be "baptized in the Holy Spirit". Our pastor felt the pressure to resist the inroads Pentecostalism was making in the church and preached several times on the topic of the correct interpretation of "tongues" in the Bible. He held that these were always languages, not gibberish. Many of our most zealous members became disturbed because of this; some even left our fellowship. Down the street the Church on the Way, a Foursquare Church, received many of these people. Still others, those who wanted more in-depth teaching than preaching on Sunday mornings, decided to join Grace Community Church, where John MacArthur had a strong teaching ministry.

The divisions in our church resulted in Dr. Fickett's resignation. He thought he had brought First Baptist as far as he could, and so he accepted an invitation to become president of Barrington College in Barrington, Rhode Island. Our church then went through an interim period, during which it searched for a new pastor. The congregation was looking for a dynamic speaker with a charismatic personality, one worthy of a large Baptist church such as ours. Throughout this period, we were continually losing members to the churches I mentioned above. Times were not so full of joy now; some members were becoming demoralized. Finances were becoming more of a problem. The feeling of expectancy, that God was working in our church, was gradually being lost.

Eventually, the church called Dr. Jess Moody from Florida as the new pastor. In spite of his bubbling personality, many people were unable to accept his leadership, and he was hard-pressed to keep a positive spirit alive in the church. A big split occurred, and about one thousand people left to form a new fellowship. Several years later they were able to convince Dr. Fickett to come and join them as their pastor.

Monique gave birth to a girl on September 11, 1975, and she was a little blondie. We named her Mireille. I had known someone by that name at Bethel in Paris. It means *Mary* in Provençal, a dialect of southern France. We began looking for a house to buy, but there was nothing within reach of our budget in the San Fernando Valley. Eventually, we found a house in Saugus, not far from Los Angeles Baptist College and Ed Gruss. My parents loaned us the down payment, and we ended up with a monthly payment that was less than what we had been paying for our apartment! When Mireille was five months old, Monique became pregnant again. This presented a complication.

For the previous six months, I had been corresponding with a missionary in southwestern France. He wanted to know if I would consider taking over his work for a couple of months so that he could visit his supporting churches in the States. His letter, combined with the problems at First Baptist, motivated us to consider entering missionary work in France. We had begun making inquiries and had become more serious about the idea when we found out Monique was pregnant again. Going to France would have to wait until Monique had the baby. But the waiting was beneficial, because it gave us a good opportunity to pray and to investigate various mission boards. When the time arrived, Monique gave birth to our second son, Daniel Christian. Because our missionary acquaintance in France was working with the Capernwray Missionary Fellowship of Torchbearers, we decided to find out more about them. We learned that it was an interdenominational work that had training centers for young people. An Englishman, Major Ian Thomas, was the founder of the Torchbearers. He is a dynamic speaker and has authored several books about the blessings of living a Christ-centered life, meaning a *Spirit-filled* life.

Major Thomas' teaching has nothing to do with the present-day charismatic movement, but his message deals principally with the victorious Christian life. His movement seems to be an outgrowth of the Keswick Conventions in northern England.[2] Those who have read the books of Andrew Murray or John E. Hunter will know what I am talking about. It seemed to us that Major Thomas' teaching offered the proper balance as well as a good response to Pentecostalism. I was also interested in the writings of Francis Schaeffer, a Protestant scholar who founded l'Abri, a community in Switzerland. His desire to follow the Holy Spirit's direction impressed me a great deal. These influences led us to seek membership in an interdenominational work rather than in a Baptist mission. Although I considered myself to be a strong Baptist, Monique and I desired more liberty to follow the leadings of the Holy Spirit. Because of our past experience with Jehovah's Witnesses, it seemed a good idea to avoid a narrow, denominational mission that would seek to impose its views upon us.

Since we needed to become better acquainted with the Torchbearers, we decided to attend a conference they were sponsoring in the San Diego area. Listening to Major Thomas speak, I was very impressed by his spirituality. Later, we spoke with him about our desire to visit France in 1977 and after-

[2] "Keswick Convention. An annual summer gathering of evangelical Christians, held since 1875 at Keswick in the Lake District of nothern England. . . . From the beginning the convention has had as its aim the deepening of the spiritual life . . . where defeated and ineffective Christians may be restored to spiritual health. . . . Among the better known [speakers] are Donald G. Barnhouse, F. B. Meyer; H. C. G. Moule, Andrew Murray, John R. W. Stott, Hudson Taylor, and R. A. Torrey." S. Barabas, in *Evangelical Dictionary of Theology*, ed. Walter A. Elwell (Grand Rapids: Baker Book House, 1984), pp. 603–4.

ward attend the Torchbearers' international conference in England. I told him we didn't have the money for such a trip, but that we were praying about it. I remember well his saying to me: "If God wants you to go, you'll go, and it won't be anything difficult. Water cuts its own channel, and so does the Holy Spirit. If God wants you to go, he will make it possible." That was encouraging but seemed easier said than done.

To our great surprise, we were able to go to France and to northern England to attend the conference. Our closest friends were aware of our desires and objectives, and two couples from our church provided the money for the trip. Even baby Daniel, who was only a couple of months old, became an international traveler because he was too young to be left with someone else.

While in Biarritz, France, where we were considering working, I had an experience that would have a great impact on our lives many years later. I had an opportunity to witness to a Catholic who had an interest in the cults and knew something about the Jehovah's Witnesses. He asked me if I would be interested in visiting a nearby Benedictine monastery and sharing my experience with the monks. What an opportunity, I thought. God is giving me the chance to evangelize Catholic monks! He called the brothers, and they were agreeable that I come and talk to them.

We drove to Notre-Dame de Belloc, about thirty kilometers from Bayonne. As we approached the monastery from a distance, I saw that it was situated on the top of a hill, surrounded by verdant countryside. Drawing closer, I could see whitewashed buildings with red-tiled roofs. When we arrived, we were greeted by the *hôtelier*, the monk who receives the guests. He offered us a little glass of white wine in a sign of hospitality and friendship, which, of course, I, being Baptist, felt obliged to refuse. (This refusal is usually not understood in France and therefore is not appreciated.)

I spoke for about fifty minutes to the assembled monks,

and, as I was concluding, I tried to stress the necessity of accepting Jesus as Savior and trusting him alone for salvation. I realized I was being a little brazen, but, I thought, it's a once-in-a-lifetime opportunity; make the most of it. Father Marc, the *hôtelier*, said to me as we were leaving, "Thanks a lot for coming, and let's remain in *union de prière*"—meaning, let's remember one another in prayer. That's fine with me, I thought; I'll pray hard that God convert you. As it turned out, we maintained contact with each other over the next nine years. I had no idea then of the friend he would become and the important role he would play in my life.

We returned to California with hearts filled with joy, but something seemed to nag at my heart about going to work in Biarritz. Believing that God was calling us, I suppressed my doubts because I was determined to get to work to raise the needed funding to enable us to live and work in France. But we had already learned an important lesson: God would provide. In November 1977, we attended another Torchbearer conference in San Diego, where we enjoyed listening once again to Ian Thomas. While he was speaking about how important it is for people to allow God *to be* God, I heard very clearly within me the words: "Go. I can take care of you in France just as well as I have here." These words were so clear in my mind that we decided to leave for France the following February.

Upon our return home, I informed the church that I would be leaving their employment at the end of December. We would live on our savings and on the money God was providing for our support, while I gave all my energies and time to fund-raising. A member of our missions' board told us we would need at least fifteen hundred dollars a month for our family of five. People from the General Association of Regular Baptists told me that many missionaries spend at least two years visiting churches before reaching their required financial goals. I didn't want any of that. I was anxious to go. Van Nuys pledged to give us three hundred dollars a month; that was a great start. Having chosen an interdenominational group, I found that lining up appointments for speaking was not as easy as it might have been.. We had no mission board with a denominational list of churches to contact. We totally lacked experience. Some congregations wouldn't support anyone who was a Baptist, while others disliked interdenominational works. Fortunately, we knew a lot of people, and I was known to a number of churches because of my speaking engagements and my writings. That was surely a great help in getting started. As we met more pastors and spoke to their churches, we found we were being scrutinized very closely. It became clear that it was going to be easier to get speaking appointments than to get support.

One of the problems I faced in raising funds was my leaning toward Calvinism. I was attracted to it because it seemed very logical, but it wasn't long before I learned that it was a very unpopular theory with most pastors and churches. I was not a true Calvinist, because I accepted only three of the five points that make up the system. Even though I was moving toward the fourth article, I wasn't quite convinced of it. This is still too much for most churches, yet it isn't enough for real Calvinists! After speaking in a Baptist church in San Diego, I wrote that church a letter in which I innocently wrote "in his sovereign grace", before signing my name. This was enough to lose any consideration for support. Regardless of these issues, the churches we visited never failed to pay for our traveling expenses and to provide a check either from a special collection for us or from their speakers' fund.

After only a few months, our fund was growing, and it was time to make preparations to leave. There was so much to do and seemingly so little time. We saw we needed a good dose of perseverance in order to overcome the pressures and uncertainties. We would have to sell the house, the car, and most of our furniture and appliances. We would only take a few furnishings and my library of a thousand books to France. Judd, one of the church's staff members, was very helpful in getting the house ready for sale. He did some touch-up painting, and Dave, another generous friend, installed new carpeting in the house for us at his own expense. When the house was ready to be put on the market, it was January 1978. Next, we applied for our visas, contacted a mover, and began thinking about scheduling a flight to France.

We quickly learned that perseverance was a very necessary quality. Without it, we could succumb to the pressures and uncertainties. The week before our departure, we were worried. Only one-third of our support had been raised, our house had not yet cleared escrow, and our visas had not yet arrived. Just when our resolve was being tested most, we received a comforting sign from the Lord. The Friday before our scheduled flight out of Los Angeles on Monday, the telephone company was to disconnect our line. The last call Monique received was from the French consulate, informing her that our visas had arrived. She rushed over to the consulate in Beverly Hills and obtained our visas just minutes before it closed for the weekend. We rejoiced in God's timing and knew in our hearts that we were to press forward with our plans.

Our time in California would later be treasured as one of the happiest periods of my life. I had had the privilege of seeing many people place their faith in the Lord Jesus Christ. I had regularly visited and comforted the sick, and many of them had also strengthened my faith. I had learned much from the teaching at Van Nuys First Baptist and my theological courses. I had enjoyed the fellowship of many, especially our best friends, Phil and Marvella, who were a spiritual and financial support for many years. Other couples and individuals had helped us along the way, like Dean and Sara, Professor Gruss, and my boss, Ed Kriz. Monday, March 12, we left the States as scheduled, clinging to God's promise to take care of us. We had no idea that a long period of trials, learning, and growth lay ahead. They would teach Monique and me to depend even more upon the Lord and his wisdom (Prov 3:5).

CHAPTER 12

Baptist Missionaries in France

We arrived in France with three young children, one of whom was not yet walking. We rented a car at the Paris airport and, for the second time, followed the national highway (N10) south to Bordeaux and on to Biarritz. We entered Biarritz in a cold, drizzling rain, so typical in March, that explains why the Basque region is so green. We eventually found a house to rent in St. Pierre d'Irube, in the countryside, where we awoke in the morning to the crowing of roosters.

Though many Baptist people and several Baptist churches were supporting us, we discovered we wouldn't really be working to build a Baptist church. We were cooperating in an interdenominational fellowship called The Bible Center for the Basque Coast. Some of the people who were attending had been baptized as Catholics, Anglicans, or Presbyterians. In fact, one member of our team was a Quaker, and she had never been baptized. (Quakers don't practice baptism.) Some of us believed in "once saved, always saved", while others rejected this teaching. Germans and Austrians came to help during the summer evangelism campaign, and they were Lutherans. Almost immediately it became clear that we would not be able to impose the Baptist practice of basing church membership on baptism by immersion.

Intercommunion was the established practice at the Center. It was kind of a "fellowship"; still, they had communion services without a church actually having been formally organized. So everyone who attended our services, even visitors, expected to receive communion. During the absence of my partner (the senior pastor), I explained that it was proper for them to desire to receive communion, but I also told them that they should understand that baptism precedes communion. Therefore, if someone hadn't been baptized by immersion in a scriptural church, he should refrain from coming to the communion table. When the senior pastor returned, he heard about what I had said, and he wasn't pleased. It seems I had offended some of his longtime friends.

There were already other Protestant churches in Biarritz —Plymouth Brethren, Pentecostal, and Anglican. A couple of kilometers away, in Bayonne, there was the Reformed Church (known in the United States as the Presbyterian Church) and an English Baptist pastor who was struggling to start a church. So there we were, all of us competing with one another for members. Of course, these new converts were expected to come mostly from the Catholic population. Catholics were considered fair game. We didn't believe they were *saved*. That's why we had come to France, a Catholic country. No, a saved Catholic would be a rare item. It might be possible by God's infinite grace, but it would be wrong for a Catholic who truly trusted Christ for his salvation to remain in the Catholic Church, because of her idolatry and false doctrines. These opinions constituted the basis for evangelizing Catholics, with whom we wanted to build "New Testament churches" founded upon "biblical principles".

By the time summer arrived, several things were bothering me, and I was looking and praying for a sign from the Lord that might help me decide what to do. Summer was devoted mainly to evangelism, and it was also when we received a number of volunteers from other countries. The weather was good, and the town was full of tourists to evangelize. Biarritz is a tourist spot in the southwestern corner of France, and there are nice beaches all the way to the Spanish border. We visited homes in the villages, sang in the streets, and held meetings and "coffee bars" in the evenings. Sometimes we showed Billy Graham or Moody Bible Institute of Science films.

A decision was made to conclude our summer campaign with a Sunday morning communion service. I wondered whether this was a good idea, but our pastor wanted to emphasize the "oneness of the Body of Christ", the communion we enjoy as Christians, without regard for the denominations of which we were members. So there we were—Lutherans, Baptists, Anglicans, Reformed, Quakers, and so forth—all gathered in the meeting place. I was feeling edgy, because I was wondering whether I should participate or not. I was praying about it, when the pastor's words broke in on my train of thought. He said that he knew of a case during the war when a navy chaplain at sea didn't have any grape juice for the communion service. He used orange juice instead, reminding the sailors that the juice was only a symbol. Next, the pastor explained that, unfortunately, someone had drunk the grape juice the night before. Having just discovered this before the church service, he decided that he had a similar emergency on his hands and that we would have apple juice for communion. He told us to remember that this would symbolize the blood of Christ. This, I believed, was my *sign*. I whispered to Monique, "Let's get out of here." And so we got up and left.

That evening I called my mission partner. He asked me why I had left in the middle of the morning service. After I explained what I felt, he informed me that I had no reason to be upset. The group ended up serving wine for communion because a visiting French Baptist, upon hearing of the problem, went out to his car and got a bottle of wine he had in the trunk. So the pastor was obliged to use wine, which normally he wouldn't do because he was a Baptist from America. Secondly, he said that I was too sensitive about this because I had been raised a Catholic and had believed communion to be a sacrament.

After six months, we left the Bible Center and associated with the Brethren group in Biarritz. I knew we needed fellowship, and I wanted very much to be part of a French assembly. Since I realized I still had much to learn about evangelizing in France, I wanted to be immersed in a French cultural situation. The Brethren manifested a strong sense of worship and took their faith very seriously. I admired their humility and the love they evidenced for the Lord.

During our year in the Biarritz-Bayonne area, I began examining my position on ecclesiology. Since I was able to fix my own schedule, I continued my morning practice of daily Bible reading—this allowed me to read the Bible through in a year—but I now added another two or three hours for research. I chose a subject and read everything I could find that related to it; I didn't worry about how long it might take. If I spent several months on a subject, what did it matter? I studied the Baptist Church and its history and the differences between the Brethren and the Baptists. I even read some books and magazines on Catholicism, because I wanted to document its weak points. The afternoons and evenings were reserved for visiting people and attending meetings.

In my research, I came across the testimony of a Catholic woman who had been raised a Protestant. In her book she gave several quotations from the early Church Fathers regarding the Eucharist and baptism. It seemed incredible that such statements could be found so soon after Christ's death. I wanted to see them for myself and to check their context. I went to Notre-Dame de Belloc, where the monks graciously let me use their library. After examining the quotations, I meditated on what I had read and the possible choices open to me. Had these documents been tampered with? Were these glosses, which were later considered to be part of the original writings? If these were accurate records of statements made by disciples in the second century, then they would be strong evidence for the apostolic nature of the Catholic Church. I wondered how it could have been possible for these Christians to have become so superstitious at such an early date; how could they have so easily changed the ordinances into sacraments? *This had to be the case.* I was trained to reject any testimony outside the Bible. If I didn't, I realized I might be led to accept such ideas as baptismal regeneration and transubstantiation. So I dropped the matter like a hot potato, as unsolvable and unthinkable.

I was invited to attend the ecumenical meetings held at the Catholic Seminary in Bayonne. I accepted the invitation to represent the Baptist position. I was happy to have this opportunity to meet people interested in God's Word. One evening, before the meeting began, I was invited downstairs, where there was a private chapel. I sat there praying while the priest and others also prayed silently. I prayed that God would help me uphold my position on baptism, the topic for our meeting. As I sat there, I watched the seminarians entering the chapel from the side and genuflecting before a large crucifix. Their gesture was so reverent, so unrushed. As they bent their knees before the Savior, I watched them make the sign of the cross, bowing their heads. It was very moving. Their reverence for Christ impressed me very much. The memory would remain engraved in my mind years later.

After spending a year in the Basque region, we decided to move about a hundred kilometers farther east to Oloron-Ste-Marie, just south of Pau, in the rural area called the Béarn. After three months of searching, we found a large, two-story, four-bedroom house in Moumour, a village of seven hundred inhabitants. One of the bedrooms could be used as an office. The big living room could be used for Bible studies. The house had a garden with two apple trees. We had a barnlike structure that could be used as a garage and for storing fuel for the wood-burning stove. The house was more

*Monique teaching a Bible study class to children in our home
in Moumour (Oloron-Ste-Marie), France*

than 150 years old. It had stone walls about two feet thick. The roof was high and covered with slate shingles, typical of the region. Across the street from the house was a large campground with giant oak trees. Beyond that flowed a river, which could serve for baptisms. Yes, we would be very happy during the five years we lived there.

We started out holding Sunday morning services in our home. At that point, we avoided giving any denominational coloring to our work. We didn't advertise that we were Baptists, because we wanted to conform to the nondenominational work of the Torchbearers, as we had been personally instructed to do by Major Thomas. We even invited the local priest to the house to see a film.

I set up a literature stand at the outdoor market in Oloron, placing stacks of New Testaments, Bibles, and other books and tracts on a table. I used a large umbrella to protect the literature from the sun and the rain. I set out placards and invited people to read the Bible and to receive Jesus as Savior. These are methods evangelicals use in France, but the response wasn't very good. Most people walked by without even giving us a glance. Nobody wanted to show any interest; so many knew each other or were related. People weren't willing to risk breaking the family unity by changing religions. Besides that, they were plainly just not interested.

I thought it would give us more status if we had a meeting place in Oloron (population 8,000) where we could use the window for advertisements. We located something about the size of an office. We painted it and put up a sign that read: *The Bible Center*—a nondenominational name frequently used in France. This should be good, we thought; it will identify us as people who love and believe in the Bible. We announced our meetings in the papers: Bible studies, movies, special speakers. We even organized a big public exposition on the Bible and invited the town's dignitaries. We sought friendship and cooperation with the Christian and Missionary Alliance work in Pau (a town of about 125,000) and with the Brethren throughout France. We eventually had a group of about ten people, including my family. This wasn't much, but they agreed to organize as a church body under the name "Bible Baptist Church".

Monique began her own ministry. She invited the children's friends to come to our house for Bible classes. The schools in France have an arrangement with the Catholic Church that gives the children in the lower grades Wednesday off from school. They go to school Saturday mornings to make up the time. The Church uses Wednesdays to conduct catechism classes for the children under twelve years of age. A little group of children (mostly gypsies) attended Monique's classes. After about six months, opposition from the parents put a stop to the Wednesday classes. The children had to attend catechism at the Catholic Church so they could make their first communion. Traditionally, this is a very important event in France. It seemed to us that for most French Catholics it was just a cultural thing.

In our eyes the people seemed to be very poor Christians, if we could call them that. They went to Mass when they had to; they attended weddings, baptisms, confirmations, and funerals at the village or town church; but mostly, they went about their business of farming or whatever, never seeming to give God any importance in their lives. God was there *if* they felt the need, but it didn't seem as though they felt the need very often.

Those who are devout and regularly attend Church are a small minority in France (5 to 8 percent). What is surprising is that so many of the French have taken up with astrology, reincarnation, yoga, and other esoteric ideas. New Age literature fills the bookstore shelves. Many admit to being atheists. No doubt the history of the country explains the low esteem the people have for the institutional Church. The Second Vatican Council seems to have had an adverse effect on many Catholics in France, perhaps because those who attend Mass (or used to) are conservative and traditional. This told us something about the mentality of the people we had chosen to evangelize. Even though the majority of French people don't practice their religion much, they still consider themselves to be Catholic and so remain extremely wary of American Protestant sects.

Eventually, I began to see a need to unite with Baptists who took a much stronger position on separation from other Baptists, who were ecumenical-minded. First, reading more about the history of the Baptists and fundamentalism helped me to understand better why Baptists had divided so often. I now felt I should stand with Baptists who were more separatist. Second, evangelizing the French was not an easy task, and it didn't take long before I realized that teamwork was indispensable if we were to be successful. This is why I decided to seek fellowship with a Baptist mission. Didn't we Baptists have a scriptural basis for everything we did? And didn't we have the best form of church government?

The news from California wasn't good. I was disappointed with the direction Van Nuys First Baptist Church was taking. I knew it would be more satisfying to fellowship with people with whom we shared the same goals and ideals. I realized too that I would have to move my church membership to another Baptist church if I were going to seek membership in the type of mission I was considering. So we decided to leave the Torchbearers' Fellowship, which had been our sponsor. It was 1981 and time to return to the United States to apply to a Baptist mission agency. We decided to try Baptist Mid-Missions, which had a rather long history in France and stood for the same principles we did. We knew quite a bit about them because of our friendship with their missionaries in France.

Just before we left for the States, I attended a Baptist conference in Paris at which I met a preacher from the southern

United States who would become a good friend. Right away we felt a certain kinship because of a common interest in Bible translations and in founding strong Baptist works in France. After the conference, I accompanied my new friend, Gerald, to Saint-Chamond to meet his wife and children and to see his meeting place. He then traveled back with me to preach to my congregation. On the way, I learned that Gerald represented a Baptist church that espoused ideas known as Landmarkism.[1]

Not all Independent Baptist churches hold to the ideas labeled Landmarkism, but many do. Just as the Catholic Church says the Church has four marks—one, holy, catholic and apostolic—some Baptist churches say there are certain landmarks that mark the boundaries of a true Baptist church. Reading the books Gerald loaned me, I learned that these Landmark ideas, although strict, narrow even, could put an end to the confusion I had seen in our churches over baptism and the Lord's Supper. Although at the time I did not accept the solutions offered by these books, I could see they were logical.

When the school term ended, we flew to Chicago, where Monique's sister lived. After a brief visit, we left the children with her and took the train to Cleveland, Ohio, where Baptist Mid-Missions' central offices were located. After the necessary medical exams, we left immediately for a BMM international conference in Pennsylvania. Our next step was

---

[1] A discussion of Landmark Baptist ideas can be found in the following publications: B. B. Ray, *The Baptist Succession: A Handbook of Baptist History* (1912; reprint, Gallatin, Tenn.: Church History Research and Archives, 1984); J. R. Graves, *Old Landmarkism: What Is It?* (1880; reprint, Texarkana, Tex.: Bogard Press, n.d.); Albert W. Wardin, Jr., *Baptist Atlas* (Nashville: Broadman Press, 1980); Robert A. Baker, *The Southern Baptist Convention and Its People 1607-1972* (Nashville: Broadman Press, 1974), pp. 203–19; Bob L. Ross, *Old Landmarkism and the Baptists* (Pasadena, Tex.: Pilgrim Publications, 1979). The last two books examine Landmark ideas critically.

to travel to Cedarville, Ohio, where missionary candidates spend two weeks in classes learning the policies and practices of the mission. After the graduation ceremony we received our commissions, and we were now members of BMM.

Then the time for deputation began. Deputation is the term missionaries use to describe their fund-raising work. We went first to El Cajon (near San Diego) to transfer our church membership. Then we began visiting the Baptist churches in California. We needed to replace most of the churches that had been supporting us for the past two years, because they were definitely not interested in supporting fundamentalist Baptist missionaries. Our time was rather limited because we had to get back to France so the children could return to school. Our support was coming in slowly but surely, so BMM authorized us to return. We landed in Paris about the week before Christmas.

I took up again where I had left off in my studies of the Baptist principles I had been examining before I went to the States. I was becoming more concerned with the question, "Which Church did Christ establish?" Was it Catholic, Reformed, Lutheran, Baptist, Pentecostal, or what? Finding a date for the founding of most of these groups is an easy matter, I thought. Only the Catholic Church and the Orthodox Church appear to have any real claim to antiquity. But I assumed these Churches didn't merit investigation. Every *Protestant* knows that. Whereas most prefer to ignore such questions, I knew I could not be satisfied until I found the truth. I longed to belong to the Church that Christ established.

During 1982 we had the opportunity to visit several times our friends near Lyons, who lent me magazines from the churches holding Landmark ideas. Eventually I subscribed to the *Baptist Challenge*, published in Little Rock, Arkansas. This led me to get in touch with M. L. Moser, the editor of the paper. Finally, I concluded that Jesus could have established only one church, one that would continue throughout the ages (Mt 28:19–20; Eph 3:21; 1 Tim 3:15). At the same time, I rejected the Protestant teaching that the true Church is an *invisible* Church. This is the position held by BMM. I had always been taught this, and I had taught it myself, yet now I saw that the doctrine is without scriptural support. I learned also that the word *church*, as used in the New Testament, applies 99 percent of the time to a local, visible Christian assembly.[2] And lastly, I agreed with the idea that the Church is a requisite for the transmission of truth (1 Tim 3:15).[3]

My mind was made up; regrettably, I could no longer subscribe to my mission's statement of faith, and I wanted to be a member of a *real* Baptist church. But I still had another difficult decision to make. These Independent churches baptize everyone entering their membership if he has not already been baptized in a church of "like faith and order", and the First Baptist Church of Van Nuys received members who had been immersed in other churches of other denominations. My new friends didn't consider such a church to be a regular, *orthodox* Baptist church.

Baptism by immersion is not the primary issue with these Baptist churches because even the Catholic Church has performed baptisms by immersion and still accepts the practice today. Mormons and JWs also practice immersion. The *real* issue for Landmark Baptists is *authority*. They teach that only churches that have been properly organized and that adhere

---

[2] See Edward H. Overbey, *The Meaning of Ecclesia in the New Testament* (Little Rock, Ark.: Challenge Press, n.d.); also, Willard A. Ramsey, *The Nature of the New Testament Church on Earth* (Greenville, S.C.: Hallmark Baptist Church, 1973).

[3] Presbyterian Albert Barnes admits this in his comments on this passage. "Thus it is with the church. It is intrusted with the business of maintaining the truth, of defending it from the assaults of error, and of transmitting it to future times." See the entire quotation in *Barnes' Notes on the New Testament*, ed. Ingram Cobbin, reprinted from the London ed. (Grand Rapids: Kregel Publication, 1962), p. 1142.

to Landmark principles have the authority to baptize. This stand actually leads to the conclusion that other denominations are not really *churches*, and that their ministers are not really gospel ministers.[4]

I had been less than two years with BMM, but I would have to make the adjustments required by my new convictions. This was not an easy decision; in fact, it hurt my pride. It risked making me look ridiculous in front of my friends, who would question my stability. The idea of another baptism was extremely difficult for us to accept. Monique was happy with BMM and our friendships there. Our disagreement was the hardest battle we had fought so far. We were arguing almost every day. Finally, after much debate, she agreed to follow me. Weren't my arguments biblical, logical, *and* historical? The time had come to buy tickets again for the States.

First, we flew to Atlanta, and from there we traveled by car to the Greenville area in South Carolina. We needed to get personally acquainted with the church we were planning to join. Our correspondence indicated that this church was extremely serious about practicing all they had learned from the New Testament. While we were with them, we had the opportunity to see a man excommunicated during an open meeting of the entire church. It was the first and only time I have seen this happen in a Baptist church. Even though I liked these people very much, after several long conversations with the elders, I became uneasy about continuing with them. We had differences of opinion on eschatology and some minor things, and I came to the conclusion that I shouldn't join their church. After passing a sleepless night, most of which was spent in prayer, I called Pastor M. L. Moser in Little Rock and inquired about going there and

---

[4] A. C. Dayton, *Alien Baptism* [Pedobaptist and Campbellite Immersions], preface by J. R. Graves (1858; reprint, Louisville, Ky.: Baptist Book Concern, 1903; Aberdeen, Miss.: The Baptist, 1977).

joining Central Baptist Church. So we drove out to Little Rock, Arkansas, the church paying for the car rental.

The South was totally new to us. The people are very warm, like their weather. Things seemed slow, calm, and peaceful. But the preachers were just the opposite. Some of them could really wind up. During the first service we attended at Central Baptist, Pastor Moser was preaching and shouting so loud that little Daniel covered his ears with his hands.

Pastor Moser and his congregation were very kind and hospitable. We enjoyed spending the first several weeks in the pastor's home. During a scheduled meeting, the church listened to our testimony and profession of faith and then voted to receive us as members by means of baptism. So Monique and I were baptized for the fourth time!

Later, the church voted to accept us as their missionaries to France, and they bought a secondhand car for our use in the deputation work. This time we drove through unfamiliar states and met Baptists of a different stripe. We traveled all over Arkansas, Texas, Oklahoma, Tennessee, Kentucky, Ohio, and Indiana. It was a long, hot trail for Jesus. I even preached one night in the Ozarks, down in a hollow. Then I flew alone to California to speak in churches out there.

In California, I met some of the best churches and pastors I have ever seen. In every church, I preached, gave my testimony, and answered questions. Often pastors discovered my beliefs through personal conversation; in other places there were long questionnaires to fill out. Once I made the remark that one had to be a theologian and a diplomat when answering these questionnaires. Some churches wanted to know if we listened to Western music or what we felt about women wearing pants. Almost all the churches wanted to know what we believed about Calvinism. Because we visited so many churches, I came to have a good knowledge of this particular group of churches and their people. Finally, I returned to

Little Rock for an interstate Bible conference at Central Baptist. Pastors came from as far away as California. During the conference, an ordination council was convened to examine the candidate—me! About forty pastors participated in the questioning before opening the meeting to the entire congregation. It went on for about two hours; I gave my testimony and then submitted to a long series of questions. When it became apparent that I had survived the questioning, a motion was made to the congregation that it proceed with the ordination. The motion was seconded and adopted. As I knelt on the floor of the stage, one by one the pastors filed by, laid hands on my head, and prayed for me. This was the second time I had been ordained, but I must admit it was the most sacred event of my life up to that moment. Weren't these the Lord's churches, his pastors, his people? I believed that this church, that is, in its institutional form, had existed since its founding by Jesus Christ.

The churches with which I was now associating are not part of any formal association or convention with central offices.[5] Although some Landmark churches belong to an association,[6] the churches with which I would be cooperating do not believe in associations because of a fear that they threaten the sovereignty of the local church. In spite of this

[5] As are the Southern Baptists, the Conservative Baptists or (North) American Baptists, and others.

[6] For example, the American Baptist Association with offices in Texarkana (Arkansas–Texas). "The object of the American Baptist Association as stated in their articles of agreement, 'Is to encourage co-operation and Christian activities among the churches, to promote interest in, and encourage missions on a New Testament basis among all peoples, to stimulate interest in Christian literature and general benevolence, and to provide a medium through which the churches may co-operate in these enterprises.' . . . The churches of the American Baptist Association are a progressive group. . . . They claim to be the descendants of the ancient Donatists, Waldenses, and Ana-Baptists." I. K. Cross, *What Is the American Baptist Association?* (pamphlet; Texarkana, Ark.–Tx.: Bogard Press, n.d.), pp. 2, 13.

strong, independent spirit, they have a great deal of unity of doctrine and methods.

However, over time I was saddened to realize that these churches bicker constantly over points upon which there should be some room for disagreement. For example, there were disputes over whether any Bible other than the King James Version could be used. Some believed wine should be used for communion services, and others strongly disapproved of the use of wine. Several times I heard a pastor say in a demeaning tone, "Oh, those *wine* churches". There was a lack of unanimity about the frequency of communion. Some Independent churches have communion services only once a year, which reminded me somewhat of Jehovah's Witnesses. Another similarity with the Witnesses was the refusal of some congregations to celebrate Christmas. Other points of controversy included the wearing of pants by women and the morality of men and women swimming together at pools or beaches.

The questioning over these issues was actually beneficial in that it forced me to sort out my ideas. While on deputation, I immediately discovered that Calvinism was a big issue among these churches. Actually, I preferred the congregations and pastors who were Calvinists. At this point, I had no trouble accepting four of the five points of Calvinism.[7] Many Calvinist preachers call these points "the doctrines of grace", because they don't like to be labeled with Calvin's name. "Calvin wasn't even a Baptist", they say. "He persecuted our forefathers." I was still wavering on the point regarding limited atonement (also called particular redemption). Usually,

[7] The five points of Calvinism are: (1) total depravity, (2) unconditional election, (3) limited atonement, (4) irresistible grace, and (5) perseverance of the saints. For a Calvinist's explanation of these points, see Edwin H. Palmer, *The Five Points of Calvinism*, enlarged ed. (Grand Rapids: Baker Book House, 1980). Taking a letter from each point gives the acronym: TULIP.

this is the last point anyone will adopt, because it means that Christ did not die for all, giving all an opportunity to be saved, but that he died only for those he elected (or predestined) to be saved. Whereas, from an intellectual point of view, this appeared logical and even scriptural, inwardly, instinctively, I felt it seemed too harsh. Many Baptist churches consider anyone who believes in limited atonement a very bad fellow, and they think that it is impossible for such a person to be a good missionary. They malign these good missionaries by saying the missionary who is a Calvinist will just lie back and wait for God to bring the chosen ones to him. This is completely false. Some of the greatest Baptist preachers and missionaries have been complete Calvinists.

These areas of disagreement did produce bitterness and strife among the Independent churches, which all claimed to have the truth. Some of them are nicknamed "Baptist Bride Churches" because they go so far as to claim that only those churches that subscribe to these tenets will make up Christ's Bride.[8] In spite of this, I admired my new friends as some of the best Christians I had ever met. They were extremely outspoken in their denunciation of ecclesiastical compromise; they were upright, honest, and sincere. I have great respect for them.

While in the United States we prayed much about where in France we should work, and it became clear to us that we should move to Perpignan. We had never visited the city, although we had driven past it on the *autoroute* to Barcelona. Perpignan is about thirty kilometers from the Spanish border and just 185 kilometers north of Barcelona. There are many Spanish immigrants there, and the region has a Catalan heritage. We planned to cooperate with missionaries in Spain and with Gerald, who was still in Saint-Chamond.

---

[8] This is an extremist position, and I don't think I have known personally any of these people, though I did discuss it once with a pastor in Kentucky who asked my opinion about it.

In 1983, we returned to France again in time for Christmas. At the sight of my trunks full of books, the customs officer said to me: "What is this, a moving?" I was bringing back a lot of old Baptist books that I had found in reprint editions and some more Bible commentaries. After we finished celebrating Christmas and putting the house in order, I went to Perpignan to look for a place to live. Available housing was scarce and expensive, so I saw it would take a while. Meanwhile, we let go of the *Centre Biblique* in Oloron, and I began devoting more of my time to translation work and preparing our next move. I had more freedom now to respond to some speaking invitations in other cities.

Time was passing; spring was drawing near, and we were still in Moumour. We went back to holding Sunday services in our home, which were attended by a retired schoolteacher from Pau and a young man from Tarbes named José, who asked to be baptized. He had come to accept the Baptist principles we were preaching. Previously, he had been a member of a minuscule Baptist church in Tarbes that was without a pastor. So we scheduled a baptism for our son Jean-Philippe, then twelve years old, and for José.

Gerald and his family came down from the north, and another missionary friend came with a group from Barcelona to attend the baptism. We decided to perform the baptisms in the river that flows through Moumour. It was only a hundred meters from our house. It was springtime, and the small river was mostly melted snow from the Pyrenees. I waded out into the middle and waited there with freezing water flowing quickly above my waist. José came out first, and I baptized him by immersing him completely in the water as I pronounced the sacred formula, "Upon your profession of faith in Jesus Christ as your personal Savior, I baptize thee, José, in the name of the Father, and of the Son, and of the Holy Ghost." Then Jean-Philippe waded out, hesitantly, eyes wide and rolling with fear. José remained beside me to help with

Ken baptising by immersion in the River Vert, France

my son. We took a position on each side of Jean-Philippe, and then we "buried" him under the waters so that he could become identified with the burial and resurrection of Christ his Savior. During the baptisms, about fifteen people who were observing from the river's edge sang a hymn. Passersby on the bridge stopped to watch the ceremony. We baptized four people in this river during the five years we worked in this area. From a human standpoint, it was not much, but having become more realistic in our expectations since we first came to France, we accepted it without any regret.

Finally, I found an apartment right across the street from the university in Perpignan. The area is called Moulin-à-Vent and is a large complex of apartment buildings on the southern edge of town. Perpignan has a population of about

120,000 and so seemed to offer better prospects than Oloron-Ste-Marie. The town already had a large Pentecostal church, a sizable Mormon chapel (called a Ward in the United States), and a very small fundamentalist Baptist church. But these Baptists received people who had been immersed by non-Baptist churches, so we proudly considered ourselves the only *real* Baptists in Perpignan. We could surely expect God's blessing on our mission.

José wanted to be a member of a *sound* Baptist church, so he decided to join us and help us build a church. We told him that he was welcome to live with us and that we would share everything with him. The apartment was much smaller than our house in Moumour, and many of our belongings (and worse, books!) had to be stored in the basement. The storage area was packed to the ceiling, blocking the entrance so we couldn't get in to search for anything we needed. We realized that we needed an office downtown for our meetings. It would be a while before we could find and open such a place.

The first Sunday after our arrival, we went for a ride to see the area. As we drove, we looked for a convenient place to hold a little service. Spotting a gravel pit on the road to Font-Romeu, we pulled in and held our first meeting. As we sat there on a pile of gravel, we prayed and sang hymns, and I gave a short Bible message. Until we found a meeting place downtown, we held Tuesday night Bible studies and Sunday services in our apartment.

After weeks of searching, we found an inexpensive, second-floor office for rent in the center of town. José, Jean-Philippe, Monique, and I washed and painted the place, which apparently had been empty for some time. We thought it was pretty nice when we were finished. We had a living room for informal gatherings and a hall for meetings, and I even had a small office for my studies and translation work.

One of my first goals was to make available several sound Baptist booklets for our evangelization work. So I set to work translating into French two large booklets and two tracts, which I eventually published on my own little duplicator. Besides these I translated into French a booklet on the local church for the American Baptist Association in Texarkana (on the Arkansas-Texas line). All the while I continued working on a catechism of Baptist doctrines. As soon as I had a chapter translated into French, we would study it on Sunday evenings.

One of the booklets we published discussed the meaning of *ecclesia* (Greek for assembly, or church) in the New Testament. But *The Trail of Blood* was our most important project. This small book traces Baptist history from the time of Christ down to our present day, identifying true Christians as the ones called Montanists, Donatists, Bogomiles, Albigenses, Anabaptists, and so on. At various times in Church history, it argues, the only glimpse we have of true Christians is a trail of blood, because the Catholic Church persecuted these groups.[9] When I had finished and corrected the manuscript, I mailed it to Pastor Moser, who did the typesetting in Little Rock. He then sent me the proofs, which I corrected and returned to him.

We printed five thousand pieces of promotional literature on our duplicator, which we then distributed to all the mailboxes in the Moulin-à-Vent area. We expected good results, because about fifteen thousand people inhabited this apartment complex. We got one reply. It was from a single lady who had two small children and a lot of personal problems. We were disappointed, to say the least.

We advertised our films, public conferences, and special events in the newspapers. One couple from Spain came for a while before they moved to another country. One day a young couple with a baby walked in the door. Jacques and Chafia had seen our sign outside, and curiosity had brought

---

[9] Meaning "Baptist Christians".

them in. At one time, Jacques had been a Baptist in Perpignan, but he had since become inactive. His wife, of Algerian and Moslem parents but born in France, was very intelligent but critical. Eventually, we were having from six to twelve persons at the meetings, but we never established a church in Perpignan. Things were going to take an unexpected turn.

PART FOUR

Full Circle: Back to the Catholic Church

And he arose and came to his father. But while he was yet at a distance, his father saw him and had compassion, and ran and embraced him and kissed him. And the son said to him, "Father, I have sinned against heaven and before you; I am no longer worthy to be called your son." But the father said to his servants, "Bring quickly the best robe, and put it on him; and put a ring on his hand, and shoes on his feet; and bring the fatted calf and kill it, and let us eat and make merry. For this my son was dead, and is alive again; he was lost, and is found." And they began to make merry.

—LUKE 15:20-24

CHAPTER 13

A Baptist Examines His Bible

We never held a communion service at the Baptist mission in Perpignan. Our particular Baptist beliefs required that the mission be organized first as a church before the Lord's Supper could be celebrated. This meant that if we should spend five or ten years in the field without being able to establish a church, we couldn't celebrate the Lord's Supper, because the Lord's Supper is a church ordinance. Even though I understood the reasoning behind this, it was a great sacrifice for any Christian to make. As time passed, I began reflecting more thoughtfully on our situation. Here we were, Americans in France and very strict Baptists, so rigid that we were not permitted to cooperate with other Baptists. We insisted on stringent requirements, some beyond reason: no wine, no pants for women, short hair for men, rebaptism for all who joined our church. I was beginning to think that we were not much different from an invading virus. We were pushing nonessential Protestant ideas and American culture on Catholic Frenchmen in the middle of a huge wine-producing region. Our kind of Baptists went so far as to refuse to believe that Jesus turned water into wine at the marriage feast of Cana. They claim he turned the water into grape juice (I never believed this). Clearly many who qualified (by God's grace) for entrance into heaven would never qualify for membership in the church we hoped to found. For example, Jacques was a jazz musician and often played in nightclubs to earn a living. Though he attended our meetings, we could not allow him to become a member of the church. I began to feel boxed in, and I wondered if I hadn't painted myself into a corner. Were all our requirements true and necessary? I began to wonder.

Gerald had had reprinted in the States the old Protestant Bible translation, revised by J. F. Ostervald,[1] so that we fundamentalists in France would have a Bible that followed the Received Text, as did the King James version. Since biblical Greek interested me a great deal, I thought it would be a good idea to translate at least the Gospel of Matthew into French, using the Ostervald as my basis. I set two goals for myself: adhere as closely as possible to the Greek and update the French as found in the Ostervald version only where necessary. I set up a long table under a large skylight in the hallway of my office. On this table, I spread six to eight different French and English Bibles, several Greek New Testaments, various commentaries, and Greek lexicons. The Ostervald version, like the King James version, placed in italics any words not actually found in the original language. I wanted to put all of Matthew's Gospel on a computer disk. I thought I could use it later for print-outs for group Bible studies.

As my work proceeded, I came to Matthew 3:11, "I indeed baptize you with water unto repentance." This is an important passage because it describes the baptizing work of the first Baptist![2] What intrigued me was the use of the Greek preposition *eis* ("unto" or "into"), which has a number of possible meanings. I was very interested in this because I had become quite adept at arguing the interpretation of prepositions when presenting our ideas. As I studied Matthew 3:11, several questions popped into my mind. Were all

[1] *La Sainte Bible qui contient l'Ancien et le Nouveau Testament*, d'après la version revue par J. F. Ostervald (Paris: Société Biblique et Française et Etrangère, 1838). Title page from a Bible in my library. Actually, the "Ostervald version" was a revision by Jean-Frédéric Ostervald of the old Geneva Bible, published in Neuchâtel, Switzerland, in 1744.

[2] Some Baptists trace their lineage to John the Baptist; others don't.

these intricate arguments really necessary? How did people read the Gospels in the first centuries? When they read the texts in their own language, in context, taking them at face value, did they readily think of these secondary meanings? Was it possible that we were stretching it a bit, when we used a far-removed meaning of a preposition in order to defend an interpretation peculiar to us?

My research led me to examine several passages in the Acts of the Apostles (Acts 2:38 and, particularly, 22:16). Something really attracted my attention here. Ananias, a Christian prophet, says to Paul: "And now why tarriest thou? Arise, and *be baptized, and wash away thy sins,* calling on the name of the Lord" (KJV).[3] Since I respected A. T. Robertson highly, I consulted his grammatical commentaries for an explanation. What I found was disturbing:

> Submit yourself to baptism. So as to *apolousai,* Get washed off as in 1 Cor. 6:11. *It is possible, as in 2:38, to take these words as teaching baptismal remission or salvation by means of baptism, but to do so is in my opinion a complete subversion of Paul's vivid and picturesque language.* As in Rom. 6:4–6 where baptism is the picture of death, burial and resurrection, so here baptism *pictures* the change that had already taken place when Paul surrendered to Jesus on the way (verse 10). Baptism here *pictures the washing away of sins* by the blood of Christ.[4]

I was stunned! Baptists were resorting to *picturesque language* to weaken (escape?) what is said here.

After giving the matter some thought and having consulted all my commentaries, I decided to visit the Jesuit library and play devil's advocate. I wondered how Catholics explain such passages (including Acts 2:38 and 1 Peter 3:21). I needed to consult commentaries that presented a contrary point of view. I wanted to test the strength of their argu-

---

[3] Emphasis added.

[4] A. T. Robertson, *Word Pictures in the New Testament* (Nashville: Broadman Press, 1932), 3:391–92; emphasis added.

ments, and *I wanted to be tested*. I was disappointed when I didn't find anyone at the Jesuit library who was interested in discussing this in depth with me. Not seeing any serious commentaries, I left feeling frustrated.

That very week I wrote to my friend Roy, in Martigues, France. I knew he had a reputable set of commentaries by Lenski, a Lutheran. I inquired if he would be kind enough to send me a photocopy of the commentary on Acts 22:16 from Lenski's *Interpretation of Acts of the Apostles.*[5] On page 909, Lenski says: "This is one of the cardinal passages on the saving power of baptism." He firmly takes issue with Robertson's figurative interpretation. When two great scholars don't agree, whom should we believe? Herein lies the problem with Protestantism, and *sola scriptura*, and private interpretation of the Bible. If two Baptist scholars don't agree, how can a simple man in the pew know which one is right or wrong (or if both are wrong)?

I read prayerfully and repeatedly every key passage on baptism in the Greek New Testament. As I questioned myself, I asked: How do the seemingly unclear passages stack up against the clearer ones?[6] Could baptism possibly be more

[5] R. C. H. Lenski, *The Interpretation of Acts of the Apostles* (Minneapolis, Minn.: Augsburg Publishing House, 1961).

[6] Acts 2:38 and 22:16, in the light of Mark 16:15–16, John 3:3–5, and 1 Peter 3:20–21. There are other passages that are very clear to me but may not be to other readers, so I haven't mentioned them here. I even discovered that the French *Louis Segond* version (1910 ed. and the *Nouvelle Edition de Genève 1979*) changed the word order in 1 Peter 3:21 from what it is in the Greek, with the result that the passage is weakened. This change strengthens the Evangelical Protestants' contention that baptism in and of itself doesn't do anything. The French *Scofield Reference Bible* (*Louis Segond* version, rev. 1975) is very popular among Fundamentalists, i.e., Baptists, Plymouth Brethren, and others.

Interestingly, in Acts 2:38 it translates the preposition *eis* as *because of.* "Repentez-vous et que chacun de vous soit baptisé au nom de Jésus-Christ, . . . *à cause du* pardon de vos péchés; et vous recevrez le don du Saint-Esprit." Meaning ". . . be baptized in the name of Jesus Christ, *be-*

than a symbol? Was it an efficacious sacrament? At this point I wasn't prepared to make up my mind; I merely suspected there was a possibility that I might be wrong. I concluded that it would be better to leave it for the time being. Anyway, the Catholic Church couldn't possibly be right here, could she?

While I could admit the possibility that our position was not impregnable, I still felt I could loyally continue. A crack will appear on a wall or building when the foundation is not solid and when stress is placed upon the structure. In my case, the cracking first appeared along the lines of our beliefs concerning God's coming Kingdom. After more than ten years of Bible study, I still had difficulties harmonizing certain passages dealing with Christ's Second Coming and the rapture of the Church.[7] I had previously managed to suppress my suspicions that the Baptist teaching on this might be wrong because there were plausible arguments that seemed to prove the doctrine, and I thought one should follow the *experts* when in doubt. However, as I continued searching the Scriptures, several things did not fall into place very well. It was at this point that I read a book, written during the last century,[8] that prompted me to reexamine completely the subject of Christ's Second Coming. I began by marking every use of

---

cause of the forgiveness of your sins." This is definitely commentary, not translation. It shows the extent to which some will go in order to avoid the plain sense of Scripture.

[7] According to our brand of Baptists and several other groups, when Jesus returns for his Church, he *snatches it out and away* from the earth; this doctrine is called the rapture. I learned later on that the Darbyists (Plymouth Brethren) were the ones responsible for the schema most Baptists follow in their teachings on the Church, Israel, the Kingdom, and the Second Coming of Christ.

[8] J. R. Graves, *The Work of Christ in the Covenant of Redemption; Developed in Seven Dispensations* (Texarkana, Ark.–Tex.: Bogard Press, 1883; reprint 1971).

the word *kingdom* in my New Testament. Next, I examined all of Christ's parables and teachings on the Kingdom.

As 1985 came to an end, I finished the year as usual reading the Book of Revelation. More than ever before, it didn't fit the complicated dispensationalist interpretation I held.[9] The Apocalypse, or Book of Revelation, was given to encourage persecuted Christians. Its theme is simply this: Christ, the conquering King of the tribe of Judah, has vanquished Satan and his allies at the Cross. It seemed preferable to understand John's visions, not as linear or progressive periods in time, but rather as snapshots that repeat the same general idea, each chapter adding details in different words. I concluded finally that if one just read the Bible through without a prepared and detailed schema, he would not be a dispensationalist.[10]

Such thinking was not tolerated in our circles. I knew that if I entertained such ideas, I could no longer continue as a missionary with these Baptists. This was disturbing not only because I loved these people but also because I found it distasteful even to consider seeking some other religious affiliation; I had made enough changes. Why should I join another Protestant denomination? What would be gained

---

[9] Not all Baptists hold to dispensationalism, i.e., the belief that God's plan of salvation is divided into seven dispensations or ages.

[10] A dispensationalist believes that Christ's Second Advent will be in *two stages*: in the first stage he will come for his Bride, the Church, and seven years later, he will come again to destroy the wicked in the battle of Armageddon. Then follows a judgment to determine who will enter into the millennium (the thousand-year reign of Christ on earth). Some people even believe that Old Testament sacrifices will be restored in the Temple at Jerusalem during the thousand-year reign. Dispensationalism also makes a distinction between the Church and Israel, insisting that God always deals separately with these entities. This means that he does not deal with both groups during the same dispensation. In effect, it requires the Church to be removed from the earth (the rapture) before God will turn his attention again to Israel.

from such a step? I thought about those who shouted the loudest about faithfulness to Christ, about their Baptist churches being the true churches. These were the very ones who were first in line to condemn any Baptist brother who didn't agree with them over how to dot an "i". They were so sure they were right that they were ever ready to do battle for the truth. It occurred to me then that such a mentality was characteristic of a cult.

Reading Church history had become a hobby with me. I had read the *History of the Christian Church*, by Philip Schaff (eight volumes), as well as other shorter works. One day, while visiting a bookstore, I saw that a new history of the Catholic Church had recently appeared.[11] I decided to buy it to see what I could learn about the history of the Church in France. I read the first volume with my usual attitude, looking for statements that might prove helpful in evangelizing Catholics. By the time I finished the second volume, I had a very different impression from what I had anticipated. The first volume more or less substantiated what I believed, and I noted all the problems during the growth and expansion of the Catholic Church. At the same time I was impressed by the writer's objectivity, his frankness. I found my opinions and attitudes were evolving somewhat. Although I was not certain about the first two centuries of Church history, I now admitted that the Catholic Church had been present in every other century. I began to doubt several points in the Baptist history as written by several Baptists whom I had read. For instance, it seemed a little far-fetched to claim as their own Novatus, Saint Patrick,[12] and Conrad Grebel, one of the

---

[11] Paul Christophe, *L'Église dans l'histoire des hommes*, 2 vols. (Paris: Droguet-Ardant, 1982). Christophe is a priest.

[12] John T. Christian, in *A History of the Baptists*, 2 vols. (Texarkana, Tex.– Ark.: Bogard Press, 1922), writes about St. Patrick, "No certain data can be given concerning his beliefs. It can, however, be positively stated that he was not a Roman Catholic; and that he approximated in many things

founders of Anabaptism. Grebel, for example, baptized by pouring water on the candidate's head.[13] I had never seriously examined these points because I had had neither the time nor the desire to be so exacting; and, more important, because the Scriptures clearly seemed to teach the perpetuity of the Church founded by Christ, which, a priori, I was convinced was the Baptist church. I never, even for a moment, dreamed that the Catholic Church had any real claim to be the Church Christ founded.

Since I like books (I then had about twenty-five hundred books in my library), every once in a while I dropped by the used bookshop in Perpignan to browse. One day I came across two very old volumes entitled *Conférences sur le Protestantisme*, by Nicholas Wiseman, a Catholic cardinal. The title, the old bindings and the date (1839) attracted my attention. I thought, "I'll buy these, perhaps I'll read them some day; in the meantime, they'll look nice on the shelf alongside a couple of other rare books I have." And so they lay there untouched for about a year. It was at this time (early in 1986) that one night, looking for something to read, I picked up the first volume by Cardinal Wiseman. I was expecting to see a critique of Protestantism, but upon examining the fly leaf I discovered the full title: *Conferences on the Most Important Doctrines and Practices of the Catholic Church*, which was, in fact, the title of the book.

First, I had to wade through a seventy-page introduction by the translator, in which I learned something about the

---

the doctrines of the Baptists" (1:178). On Novatian and his clinic baptism, see p. 37; for such groups as the Montanists, the Novatians, and the Donatists, his chap. 3; also, D. B. Ray, *Baptist Succession*, chap. 28 for Novatus, his clinic baptism, and the Novatians.

[13] Christian, 1:116–17; also William R. Estep, *The Anabaptist Story* (Grand Rapids: Wm. Eerdmans Publishing Co.), pp. 10–11 and 206–7, for his rejection of successionism; see also Guy F. Hershberger, ed., *The Recovery of the Anabaptist Vision* (Scottdale, Penn.: Herald Press, 1957), p. 59.

problems of the Church in England during the centuries since the Reformation. I learned that the book I had in my hands was a translation of a series of conferences given in England during 1835. The French was very good, with just enough of a hint of antiquity to make me appreciate it all the more. My interest grew as I read on.

Eventually, I got into the conferences, which discussed the reasons some people are Protestants and others are Catholics. The Cardinal stated that the division boiled down to one major issue: a different rule of faith. I found myself agreeing wholeheartedly with the Cardinal. As I lay in bed reading, every once in a while I would exclaim, "Hey, that's a good point. He's hitting the nail right on the head." It surprised me how easily I agreed with him. I had never before seriously examined the claims of the Catholic Church to be the Church that Christ founded. For the first time in my life, I sincerely wanted to see how she defended herself. As I read on, my attention grew; especially when I came to the part that dealt with the major doctrinal points.

I was impressed by this English cardinal's scholarship. He stood in front of a Protestant audience and tackled these matters during a time when the Catholic Church was extremely unpopular; he had to be a courageous man. The introduction stated that many Protestants became Catholics as a result of these conferences. I didn't believe this would happen to me, but I was willing to give the old fellow a hearing. Could a Catholic teach something to a Baptist?

Meanwhile, I summed up my study on the Kingdom in a five-page article that I sent off to the Baptist pastors I respected most. I wanted to get some feedback and hoped to discuss it with them the next time I returned to the States. The reaction was generally positive but hesitant. One Baptist church was recalling one of its missionaries over this issue of eschatology. So its pastor advised me not to publish what I had written. The weeks were passing, and my ecclesiology was evolving somewhat. It became more evident that Baptists were *struggling* to present a line of succession through the centuries. On the other hand, Catholics had no problem tracing their history through the centuries. Nevertheless, it had always seemed unthinkable that this Church was anything other than an apostate church.

I began to discern more clearly that in some way the Kingdom and the Church were related. As I studied, I wondered if the Church might *not* be limited to a local church or assembly, as we taught. Was *church* something like the covenant people (Acts 7:38; Heb 8:8, 13) of the Old Testament, the only difference being that the Church is not limited to one race or nation? In other words, *church* should not be restricted to a local congregation, because it includes a universal people traversing twenty centuries. Could I accept the fact that the Church (made up of Christians) is imperfect and has faults because it is so much like any nation? Each nation has its moments of grandeur and glory as well as its times of failure and humiliation. We don't condemn an entire nation for the acts of some of its leaders or for the actions of a part of its people; we recognize that no nation or people has a perfect history.

God never rejected Israel during her periods of infidelity and idolatry. He purposed to bring in something better, something more spiritual, based upon a better covenant and a better sacrifice. Those Old Testament promises made to Israel were fulfilled when Jesus instituted a new covenant with his Jewish disciples on Passover night. The outlines of the relationship between the Kingdom and the Church were becoming clearer to me. And I could see that Jesus' words in Matthew 16:18–20 (concerning the Church's foundation and the keys of the Kingdom) and 28:19–20 (on the Church's commission to teach and to baptize) were important. It was becoming more and more difficult to adhere to independent Baptist views on the Church. Coming to a clearer understanding of these matters prepared me for the unexpected changes that lay ahead.

By this time I was into the second volume of Cardinal Wiseman's *Conferences*. This was getting serious. I was taken aback, perplexed; where could I find help? One afternoon, as I entered the mission, I found a note in my mailbox. It was from a local parish priest who wanted to meet me. He said he had come by several times to see me but had never found me there. The note had his phone number and asked me to give him a call. I went upstairs to my office and phoned him. We made an appointment for him to come over to see me. When he arrived, I found him to be quite different from any clergyman I had known in the past. He was wearing sandals and a short, blue habit with a hood, and he had some kind of "rosary"[14] wrapped around his wrist. He was about ten years younger than I and very outgoing. I admired his enthusiasm. Frankly, I had not felt that kind of enthusiasm for more than a year. I could tell that he was a charismatic. It was like an odor that hung about him. Yes, I liked him, and I thought, "Perhaps this is an opportunity to evangelize a priest and at the same time play devil's advocate."

I asked him to take a seat where he would be obliged to see all the books on the shelves behind me. I wanted to impress him. His first words were, "I like to talk to Calvinists." He introduced himself as Père Claude Jean-Marie, and he explained that the Church was taking a survey in preparation for the coming synod in Perpignan. He asked if I would mind answering some questions from a sheet he showed me. I thought to myself: "This is a new one, Catholics calling on me to take a survey. Why, I've done this many times when I did the Campus Crusade thing in California. Now, here I am, on the receiving end." His first question was, "What do you think of the Catholic Church?" I told him very frankly that I

---

[14] Called a *chotky*, which is used for prayer in the Eastern Church.

had a bad opinion of the Church. He asked why, so I told him. Looking for something kind to say, I told him that I appreciated the Catholic Church's fidelity to the Trinity. I told him I was sorry that I was so negative and not ecumenical but that, unfortunately, he had fallen upon some very tough Baptists when he knocked on our door. The reason for this was that we believed that Jesus had founded a church that, in all its traits, was Baptist. His reply was, "Have you ever read the Church Fathers, for instance, the apostolic Fathers?"

"Yes," I said, "but only a little." I showed him my five-volume edition with the Greek text and lots of footnotes. "It's too imposing", I explained. "I have never had enough interest to wade through all of it. I have read some of the letters, but I was mainly looking for early testimonies to the deity of Jesus Christ." He suggested I read the whole thing, adding that I should understand that the apostolic Fathers were the first witnesses to the Faith after the apostles. He assured me that I would find the major Catholic doctrines substantiated in these writings. The priest told me that a professor of patristics was giving courses at the monastery and that he would ask her to give him a couple of references that he would bring me later. He said that he would lend me the apostolic Fathers in a small edition, which would be much easier to read.

Father Claude Jean-Marie returned a couple of days later. I felt a little nervous chatting with him in my office. I was hoping nobody would drop by and find him there. He left me the book on the Fathers, and I devoured it in the next few days. I looked up the references he gave me: statements on bishops, baptism, the Church, and the Eucharist.[15] I checked them in my own scholarly edition to make sure there were no differences. It was sort of unsettling. But this time I was less inclined to draw the conclusion I had drawn

---

[15] Please see the bibliography for the apostolic Fathers.

some ten years before: "Just shows you can't believe anybody, not even the first witnesses." I was more open now, more objective, more mature. If you can't believe the first witnesses, I reasoned, whom can you believe? If God founded a Church[16] that within seventy years could be so thoroughly corrupted, wouldn't he appear to be a poor builder? This time I would give these witnesses a fair hearing, weighing carefully the reliability of their statements. After all, *they were indeed martyrs for their faith.* If I found that their testimony favored the Catholic Church, then there was good reason to believe that God had preserved the deposit of faith down to our day.

Summer vacation was drawing near, and Wiseman was really bugging me. *National Geographic* published an article on the Vatican Museum and its treasures. Those beautiful pages motivated me to make plans to visit Italy for our vacation. We would go to Rome to see the sights. We had already visited Spain and Switzerland, so, I argued, we should see something different. Inwardly, secretly, I wanted to see more of Catholicism, to visit the Vatican and investigate the archeological testimony. I wanted to discover history in a more firsthand manner. Just before we left, I called my Benedictine friend, Father Marc, to let him know I was going to Rome. He was happy to hear of it and said, "Have a good pilgrimage." I assured him I was going only as a tourist. In the background, I heard the big chapel bells calling the monks to prayer. Father Marc said, "I've got to hang up now; it's time for Mass." He didn't know it, but inwardly I was very moved. The tolling of the bells spoke to my heart, they were calling me too. Something from my childhood seemed to be stirring within me.

We left for Italy during the last week in July. As we drove past Nice and Monaco along the Mediterranean coast, I con-

[16] Acts 20:28.

tinued playing devil's advocate with Monique. The kids were counting the tunnels all the way to Florence, while Monique was plagued by my questions. What do you think about this? And what about that? How do you answer these things? What if it were true? What would we do? Should we close our eyes, refuse to search out the truth? If I did change, people would really think I was crazy, wouldn't they?

We had three great days in Rome. Because Italy was very expensive for us, we couldn't afford more time than this. We got special passes from the Vatican offices to visit the excavations underneath Saint Peter's Basilica. (I had made the acquaintance of a prefect of one of the Roman congregations, and he arranged for us to visit the ecumenical offices of the Vatican, where we obtained these passes.) God's providential grace was truly working in special ways. We visited Saint Peter's Basilica and the Vatican library, and then Monique and the kids visited the excavations and the bones of Saint Peter. I didn't accompany them on this visit because I was too tired, having already climbed to the top of the Basilica's cupola.

During my visit to the Vatican, I asked myself: "How is it that the Catholic Church exists here, one generation after another, without any breaks, and without the people protesting any drastic changes (if there had been any)?" It was simply a matter of parents transmitting the faith to their children. I had never read of any protests against innovations. If the Catholics had corrupted and perverted the faith over a period of time, there should be some record of it, I thought, yet I surely hadn't seen any.

After we arrived home, I called Father Claude Jean-Marie, and he invited Monique and me to dine with the monks at the Monastery of the Glorious Cross. I tried to decline; it didn't seem fitting for me to eat with them. But at Father Claude Jean-Marie's insistence I decided to go. Afterward, I was glad we had. Before we began eating, there were readings and the singing of Psalms. Then I was startled to hear a sort of singing prayer in tongues. So, I thought, they *are* charismatics. It seemed strange listening to Catholic monks praying like Pentecostals. They did appear to love Jesus deeply. It was a pleasant visit, but not something I cared to advertise.

I had several more meetings with Father Claude Jean-Marie before the monks left for a spiritual retreat in another monastery. We were becoming friends even though I continued playing devil's advocate. Since I had attended Catholic schools, I had some inkling how he would probably answer my questions, but I still wanted to hear his responses to biblical arguments. Claude Jean-Marie knew the Bible very well, and he gave good answers. The problem was that I found it difficult to accept Catholic explanations. The testimony of the Church Fathers interested me very much. The confusion among Protestants was intolerable to me. I was convinced that Christ had founded a Church and that it had continued through the ages. But I still had doubts and fears that originated in my lack of understanding . . . and my prejudices. "Oh, God, help me", I prayed. What about purgatory, confession, Mary, and the saints?

It was time for us to go to Cerdagne (in the Pyrenees), where we usually spent a couple of days camping at the end of summer. I brought along the second volume of Wiseman's *Conferences* so I could continue reading. I started the day with my Bible reading and then spent about an hour on Wiseman's chapter about the Eucharist. He argued his case from John 6. I was surprised to discover such a tightly argued presentation by a Catholic scholar. I had never thought they could make such a good case from the Scriptures, especially on this subject. Cardinal Wiseman's argumentation was thorough, to say the least. He examined the context, the vocabulary from the original languages; he compared Scripture with Scripture and gave the testimony from history, the Church Fathers, and so on. It was complete, solid, and convincing. I came to a decision; I must talk with Father Marc in Belloc.

I found a phone booth in the campground and gave him a call. I explained what had been going on since the last time I spoke to him. I told him: "I haven't made any decisions, but I've come to see a lot of things. I need some help. I can tell you this much: I am very open to discussing seriously with you the possibility that the Catholic Church *might be* the Church Christ founded. You mustn't tell anyone what I have just told you. I'm not yet convinced of this, and it could cause a lot of problems for me, especially for my family. Monique is very opposed to this. I am going to send you some booklets and papers on our position as Baptists, and I want you to prepare yourself by reading this material so that you will be able to dialogue with me as one who understands our position. Can I come and spend three days at the monastery? I'll need at least this much time with you." Father Marc's reply was very kind; he was happy to hear what was happening in my life. "If you need three weeks, come, by all means, and don't worry about cost! We'll be happy to receive you. I am very busy at the moment, but after September I'll have the time. Can you come in October?" I was disappointed to have to wait so long, but I was glad he would be able to receive me. Our meeting was set for October.

CHAPTER 14

The Road Home: El Camino Real

José had been living with us for about two years when he learned that, because he was returning to school, he could have his own apartment at the university. This new situation proved timely for me because of what was going to take place in the near future.

The time to visit Notre-Dame de Belloc finally arrived.[1] I didn't eat very much the day before leaving, and I slept very poorly that night. I awoke at 4:30 to get ready to leave. It's about a six-hour drive from Perpignan to the monastery, and I wanted to arrive early enough to have as much time as possible for our discussions. I took along the list of questions Monique and I had prepared. She especially wanted me to ask Father Marc how Mary could hear prayers from thousands of people at the same time and in all the languages of the world. Was she some kind of god? Monique didn't want an answer, only to confound the both of us.

When I arrived, Father Marc welcomed me and showed me to my room, a little cell with a table and a bed. Then we went into a large hall used for meetings, where there were some dining tables. We sat down at a table and placed our Bibles on it, and I took out my list of questions. Father Marc had received a copy by mail. He suggested we begin by asking the Holy Spirit to guide our discussion and our time together. Each of us would pray for help; when he prayed, he asked God to help Monique too. During my stay,

[1] October 8, 1986.

he showed great compassion for us both. His concern was comforting, and I knew that my confidence in him was not misplaced. I had known Father Marc since 1977, and we had kept in contact. Hardly a year had passed that I had not visited him.

After talking a while, he got to the heart of the matter. "Ken, we're not going to get anywhere like this. You come here with your own interpretation of Church history, your Greek New Testament and your arguments. You look at things the way you've learned them, and we look at them from another angle. It will take the Holy Spirit to show you the truth. If he doesn't, I certainly can't. Each of us thinks he is right, and it will take the Holy Spirit for you to find what you are looking for."

I knew he was right, but I felt disappointed. I had gone there for some intellectual answers, and I was being asked to give my questions to God. I knew it was possible that I was wrong. I certainly had been before. But I didn't want to make a decision about the Catholic Church based upon emotion. I was fearful of making a serious mistake that would be costly in family relationships, reputation, and livelihood.

I told Father Marc that I was ready to attend all the liturgical services except Mass. Memories of my Catholic upbringing began stirring in my heart, and I could not help but be impressed by the beauty of the services. I envied the monks' quiet confidence in God and the security they seemed to derive from their long-standing place in the bosom of the Catholic Church. They could trace their unbroken history all the way back to Saint Benedict (c. 547). No Baptist congregation could do that. I did not want to belong to a new church, I thought. I longed for a tradition, something securely anchored in time.

The first time I attended Vespers, as the monks bowed at the doxology, I stood erect with my head up, not wanting to take part any more than necessary. But, as I followed their prayers, I wondered, "Why shouldn't I bow my head to God? Why are we Baptists so stiff?" It dawned on me that Baptists had highly intellectualized their religion, whereas Catholic worship included both the mind and the body and made use of externals, such as candles, incense, water, bowing, kneeling, and making the Sign of the Cross. For the first time I noticed how these things, these actions, enable the whole man to worship God. Now I understood why many of the French people told us the Reformed church and its liturgy were too austere. Our worship did seem impoverished in comparison to that of these monks.

The second morning of my stay, during the time reserved for *lectio divina*, when the monks privately read from the Scriptures or the saints, I opened my Bible to read my scheduled section for the day. My mind was assailed with fears and doubts. How was I to discover the truth unaided, I wondered. My entire lifetime would not be long enough for me to learn everything there is to know. I realized my need for a mother, a qualified teacher, a Church with the necessary experience. Before I began to read, I prayerfully asked God to help me: "Lord, if I am going to find the truth, you will have to speak to me in a language that I understand. You are going to have to show me in the Scriptures. I am so wary of men's reasonings and my own emotions. Lord, help me, please." Then I turned to my Bible and read the following:

> As they went out of Jericho, a great crowd followed him. And behold, two blind men sitting by the roadside, when they heard that Jesus was passing by, cried out, "Have mercy on us, Son of David!" The crowd rebuked them, telling them to be silent; but they cried out the more, "Lord, have mercy on us, Son of David!" And Jesus stopped and called them, saying, "What do you want me to do for you?" They said to him, "Lord, let our eyes be opened." And Jesus in pity touched their eyes, and immediately they received their sight and followed him (Mt 20:29–34).

I was stunned. Why, here was my prayer for God to open my eyes! Was God speaking to me? But, wait a minute, I thought, this could be a coincidence. It was a shock, but maybe he was speaking to me. I would have to be careful about making decisions based upon this one incident.

The third morning, the day I was to return to Perpignan, I was more relaxed than when I had arrived. As I sat in the chapel praying, pleading with God for answers, I heard the monk read:

> And I tell you, Ask and it will be given you; seek, and you will find; knock, and it will be opened to you. For every one who asks receives, and he who seeks finds, and to him who knocks it will be opened. What father among you, if his son asks for a fish, will instead of a fish give him a serpent; or if he asks for an egg, will give him a scorpion? If you then, who are evil, know how to give good gifts to your children, how much more will the heavenly Father give the Holy Spirit to those who ask him! (Lk 11:9–13).

I knew that I was sincerely asking my heavenly Father to guide me; I wanted the Holy Spirit to reveal the truth. But was this another coincidence? I remained perplexed, worried.

After breakfast, I packed my suitcase and got ready to go. I hadn't come to any decision; I was just more open, more favorable toward the Catholic Church than when I had arrived. Father Marc came to see me before I left. I suggested we pray that I have a safe trip back to Perpignan. "Okay," he said, "why don't we repeat together the angel's salutation to Mary?" A thought flashed through my mind: "Who does he think he's fooling. He means the Hail Mary. I'm not stupid." Just as quickly, I thought, why not? It's in the Bible. So I told him to go ahead. I began repeating with him the prayer, and when he got to the second part of it, the going was a lot harder because the actual words are not taken from the Scriptures. Then Father Marc said: "Let's conclude with the sign

Ken with Father Marc Doucet, O.S.B.

of all Christians." Again, why not? And so I followed him in making the Sign of the Cross. The tears were now falling down my cheeks. I hadn't made the Sign of the Cross since I was around fifteen years old. Was I a traitor? I wondered. Had I betrayed my church, my ordination, and everyone's confidence in me?

I assured Father Marc that I would go back home and pray about what I should do. I needed time to settle this, to come calmly to a firm decision. All the way back to Perpignan I was rejoicing and singing God's praises. I arrived at the door of my apartment and immediately was awakened to reality: the battle was not finished, it was just beginning.

Monique met me at the door as I entered the apartment. The expression on her face was like that of a lion. "Well, did your *friend* Marc answer my question about Mary *from the Bible*?" she demanded to know. It wasn't so much the question but her tone of voice that set me off. She seemed so haughty, so sarcastic. Any joy or happiness at being home was lost in a flash. "*Not everything* is in the Bible", I almost shouted. I was so angry that I lost all desire to share with her how things had gone; I didn't want to talk to her at all. I decided to go to my office downtown to see if there was any mail there. Monique came along. On the way we talked a little. We got nowhere, and I was frustrated because I knew that for the first time in my life I wasn't going to be able to convince her by arguing from the Bible. If it was so hard for me, who had been raised a Catholic, to accept the Church, how could I expect Monique, who all her life had been taught the Church was Babylon, to embrace Catholicism?

As we were getting out of the car, she said something that set me off again. I slammed the car door, and I yelled at her. The only excuse I have is that I was tired. I had not slept well for the past week, I was under great strain, and I had just arrived from a long trip. I simply couldn't bear to be scorned and looked down upon by Monique, whom I loved so much. I had more training and was more knowledgeable than she, yet I couldn't give her the answers she needed. And she knew it.

I continued trying to reason with Monique and finally convinced her to read the history of the Church by Paul Christophe. History had taught me so much, I thought. Simply traveling through Europe and visiting many ancient churches had caused me to doubt the historical claims made by the Baptists. Where are the Baptist ruins? I had often wondered. Of course, the Baptists will answer that Catholic persecutors destroyed every trace of their heritage. But the more I studied history, the more unbelievable this seemed. Perhaps history would help Monique to become more objective. At least, I hoped so. Unfortunately, she read Christophe's book the way I had always done; she looked for and found the sins of the Catholic Church. When she had finished reading it, she still insisted that the Catholic Church was apostate.

Meanwhile, I met with Father Claude Jean-Marie, who encouraged me and assured me that his entire community was praying for us. This was a big comfort, because I knew that *any* victory I might have would not be "by might or by power" but by God's Holy Spirit.[2] Every day I knelt down and asked the Lord to comfort me, to guide me. For thirty days I prayed for strength, and on my birthday, November 3, I made up my mind. I would return to the Church of my baptism, no matter what it might cost. I had come full circle. I was almost home in the bosom of my Church, the Roman Catholic Church. I rejoiced, even though I knew full well that the road ahead was going to be difficult, dangerous. I could lose my entire family, I thought.

I returned to Notre-Dame de Belloc to spend another three days. Everything was very different this time. I was relaxed, and I ate better because I felt more at home. I wanted to begin right away practicing my faith, even if only in a small way. It felt good to be home, to be Catholic. This time I attended Mass with the monks. Father Marc and I had a good time, maybe even better than before, since there was less tension; we rejoiced over our spiritual blessings. He counseled me that, when I got back home, I should ask the priest in Perpignan to introduce me to the bishop.

As soon as I got back, I went to the Catholic bookstore in Perpignan and bought myself a small Jerusalem Bible, and I wrote the date inside the cover, November 1986. I went to see Father Claude Jean-Marie, and I told him what Father Marc had suggested. He said that he would be happy to set up an appointment with the bishop, Msgr. Jean Chabbert.[3] An appointment was scheduled for the end of the month. I nervously waited for the date to arrive.

[2] Zech 4:6.
[3] Msgr. Chabbert was the archbishop-bishop of Perpignan because he had been an archbishop in North Africa (in Rabat, Morocco). Normally, Perpignan has only a bishop.

Before I had left the monastery, I bought a crucifix and an icon of the Virgin Mary. At home, I hung them on the inside of the closet door. Each morning I opened the closet door so I could meditate on the icon and crucifix during my prayer time. One morning, I called my youngest son, Daniel, into the room. I opened the closet door and showed him what I had bought at Belloc. I asked him what he thought of the icon of Mary with the baby, Jesus, in her arms. Didn't it show the love and tenderness she had for him? "Oh, yes", he said. Then I explained the meaning of the crucifix, commenting that this was much clearer than the cross we used. A person hearing the gospel for the first time could visualize that Christ died for him. Did he think it was better? Yes, he could appreciate that this was better. That's all I said to him for the moment. Little did I dream then how God would lead him later on.

Near the end of November, Father Claude Jean-Marie and I went to the bishop's house, located in the poorest neighborhood in town. When we arrived, the bishop was still busy, so we were asked to wait. After a bit, Father Claude Jean-Marie asked a nun who was passing by if we could go upstairs and visit the chapel until the bishop was free. She led us upstairs, and we entered a small room. A nun was kneeling on the floor before the Blessed Sacrament, which was exposed in a very large, gold monstrance upon the altar. I hesitated; I knew I should get down on both knees and adore my God. Would I do it? Well, I thought, I've made up my mind to come back to the Church, so why not? I got down on my knees and thanked the Lord God for his mercy, for his kindness, and for his patience with me who had strayed so far from the path, from the King's Highway, from *El Camino Real*. Because of my polio-weakened legs and a lack of practice spending time on my knees, I couldn't stay very long in this position. After a couple of minutes, I had to get up and take a seat on a chair. Before seeing the bishop, I had come face to face with my Lord, had been given the time to worship him, to adore him.

The bishop met with us and had encouraging words for me. He said: "I recognize you as a Catholic in spirit, even though for the moment you are still a pastor and are not back in the Church. Don't worry about your wife; don't push her. I can't believe that the Holy Spirit, having already done so much for you, won't speak to your wife and lead her to accept the Catholic Church. You leave her alone, and let him work on her heart." I appreciated his confidence, and I was willing to let the Holy Spirit work "on the inside", but I was determined to continue working "on the outside" with my arguments. Bishop Chabbert told me to wait a year before formally entering the Church to allow my wife and children enough time to hear the Spirit's urgings. In the meantime, he said he would be happy to see me about every two weeks. I went home comforted but still worried about my family.

In December 1986, I returned to Notre-Dame de Belloc for my third retreat. I was anxious during the whole trip because I had decided that I would go to confession. It would be the first time in more than thirty years. As I drove, I kept going over in my mind what I would say, wondering how it would go. Would I have the nerve to go through with it? Yes, I thought, but it was going to be one of the hardest things I had ever done. Finally, I arrived with just a few minutes to spare before Mass would begin. I told Father Marc that I wanted to go to confession. (He already knew this because I had mentioned it in my last letter to him.) "No, you can't do that", he said. "What! Why not? I've been preparing myself for the last six hours for this. I have never heard that you could tell someone he can't go to confession; why can't I?" He explained that, when he got my letter, he had phoned the bishop in Perpignan and asked for his opinion. He was told not to hear my confession, that there must be some sort of formal reentry into the Church beforehand. I couldn't simply confess and receive Communion just like that. Even though I felt a little relieved because the stress was gone, I was disappointed. I had so looked forward to it.

I had brought a gift for the monks—a bottle of liqueur from Perpignan. The abbot came to visit me in my room and offered me something for Christmas. He gave me a precious gift, a Sunday missal in which he inscribed some words for me. Just as during my previous visits, Father Marc and I continued our discussions, and my faith and hope were strengthened. I could go home, refreshed and encouraged.

I began seeing more of Father Claude Jean-Marie, and eventually I was able to persuade Monique to talk with him. We had been arguing for some time, and her typical response to my statements was "show me that in the Bible." Then I would be angry. Finally, she said she didn't want to discuss it any more. I realized we needed someone from outside to talk with her. We met with Father Claude Jean-Marie one afternoon, and he and Monique were immediately in a confrontation. He answered her in a manner that seemed too authoritarian, and she decided she didn't want to talk with him any more. This prompted me to ask him if there were any religious sisters who could talk with Monique. Father Claude Jean-Marie informed me that perhaps someone from the Dominican sisters might be able to help. His community and theirs were good friends. He said he would try to set up an appointment for the following week. I could talk with him while Monique visited with the sister.

The appointment time arrived. Monique described to me later how it went. She said that when they began talking, Sister Martine asked Monique what the problem was, what she had against the Catholic Church. (I thought this was the worst thing she could have done.) This gave Monique the chance to say: "Everything! Mary, purgatory, the pope . . ." Then Monique went on the offensive, attacking Sister Martine for wearing a habit. She showed her Matthew 23, where Jesus talked about those who liked to parade around in long robes. They argued about Mary, too, and they both ended up crying. At the end of their meeting, Monique and Sister Martine came to see Father Claude Jean-Marie and me. He asked me to drive Sister Martine home to Ceret, near the Spanish border, because she had come on a bus.

The half-hour drive gave us a good opportunity to get to know Sister Martine a little better. She described their community. It was not old. They had left the convent and the teaching work they had previously done in order to follow closely in the footsteps of their founder, Saint Dominic. Since he had been a preacher who relied on Divine Providence, they were imitating him by living in the same manner. This gave them the freedom to preach the gospel wherever God led them. Having nothing made it easier to move about; God provided the food and the shelter.

When we arrived at the top of a hill outside of the little town of Ceret, we took a side road, at the end of which we discovered an old *ermitage*. It was a fourteenth-century Catalan chapel dedicated to Saint Ferreol. Leaving the car, we walked up an incline and met another sister, Marie-Noël. She was standing a little higher than we, the chapel visible behind her. As I gazed up at her, seeing her framed by the chapel, I felt an impulse to give her some money. So after we had talked a while and the moment arrived to shake hands, I slipped a banknote into her hand. At the moment it just seemed to be a simple way of showing some appreciation for these young women. They had left everything to follow Jesus in poverty and in the preaching of the gospel. Even though they did not possess material goods, they still had something to give: love, kindness, and a *personal* testimony of God's love, which had changed their lives and was visible for anyone to see. Monique told me that giving them money was a dumb thing to do.

Over a period of a couple of months, Monique sometimes accompanied me during my biweekly visits to the
bishop's residence. She was often antagonistic to "Father
John", as we called our bishop, but he ignored her attitude
and showed us both love and compassion. Would her heart
ever soften, I wondered.

The next important event occurred when we were invited
to visit the sisters at Saint Ferreol. I took the whole family to
spend a Saturday afternoon with them. As we sat outdoors in
the sun, we talked about Christianity, about what it meant to
us to love and serve the Lord. It seemed strange to hear
Catholic sisters talk about "the Lord" in a manner that reminded us of Evangelicals.

During our conversation I stated that I had been converted (saved) in 1973. Sister Elizabeth, who was from Bel-
gium, said, "Oh, you're converted, that's great; I don't think I
am converted yet." This seemed to be a very incongruous
remark for a Christian to make. Responding to my questioning, she explained that she thought conversion was a lifelong
experience, that over the years God would help her to continue growing in love for him and becoming more like Jesus.
At first I smugly thought that might be okay for her, but I
knew that I was converted, and I knew exactly when I had
accepted Jesus as my personal Savior. But after thinking a
little more about her statement, I recognized that we really
believed the same thing. She was just using another word,
conversion, to explain something that Baptists and Evangelicals
call *sanctification*. If I replaced her word with ours, we would
be in perfect agreement. I was beginning to appreciate that,
in many instances, Catholics and Protestants share the same
beliefs. What separates them is often nothing more than se-
mantics; they don't fully understand the other party's position because they don't use the same terminology.

We had tea and cookies with the sisters, and afterward
they invited us to stay for Vespers. I was happy for the oppor-

tunity to attend, and, since I was the driver, Monique and the children were obliged to stay. During Vespers, Jean-Philippe was looking around curiously. He seemed surprised and puzzled at his father's participation in the ceremony, but he didn't say anything. Saturday afternoon visits with the sisters at Saint Ferreol, followed by Vespers, became a regular part of our family life. As my desire for Catholic worship continued to grow, I eventually canceled the Sunday evening service at our mission so that we could visit the sisters and join them for prayer on Sunday afternoons. It did not take long for my children to become fond of the sisters and of the liturgies we shared with them.

One day I drove the family across the Spanish border to visit a beautiful Benedictine monastery called Montserrat. It is situated in a hilly region, just north of Barcelona, about a two-hour drive from our home. So many tourists visit Montserrat that the monastery has a restaurant, a post office, and a hotel. While we were seated in the restaurant, I asked Monique to take Mireille and go to the hotel and get some cash from the automatic teller machine there. I wanted to talk to my boys alone. While they were gone, I spoke privately with my sons about my decision to reenter the Catholic Church. (Jean-Philippe was about fourteen years old, and Daniel was ten.) I told them that I would not be a Baptist pastor much longer, that I had grown up in the Catholic Church and now believed she was the Church Jesus had founded. I assured them I loved them, that I was praying for them, and that I would not force them to become Catholics. I was relieved that the boys expressed no real opposition, only curiosity mixed with some doubt.

As time went on, it was interesting to note that Monique was making friends with the sisters. Sister Martine showed her much love and patience and was actually helping her grow in her understanding of the Church. Monique now accepted the sisters, and even the priests, as Christians. Finally, after several months, much prayer, and many discussions, Monique announced that she would enter the Church. I was overjoyed, but there was still a problem. She said she couldn't make the Sign of the Cross. "Monique," I explained, "that's not possible. Catholics always make the Sign of the Cross: when entering a church, when praying, and at the beginning and end of Mass." But she was adamant. She insisted she could not bring herself to do it. Father Claude Jean-Marie explained it to her, and she understood, but her upbringing and emotions still troubled her. I was obliged to let it drop. Only God could change her heart.

One evening we were invited to share a meal with the sisters at Saint Ferreol. They knew of Monique's stumbling block and had been praying for her. During the blessing of the food, I thought I caught a glimpse out of the corner of my eye of Monique making the Sign of the Cross. I did not dare ask her about it, but I wanted to be sure. After the meal, I discreetly asked one of the sisters. Yes, she also had seen Monique make the Sign of the Cross. I was so happy; I knew the Holy Spirit was at work. At last, we decided to enter the Catholic Church together as a family.

The sisters suggested that the ceremony take place at a summer camp they hold each year near Prouilhe, where Saint Dominic had founded his first convent for sisters.[4] When I spoke to Father Claude Jean-Marie about it, he didn't like the idea. He wanted us to enter the Church in the parish, in what he called a public manner. I asked the bishop, and he agreed with him. He said that we must be received by the Church in the parish and that I would have to make a public profession of faith. So the parish, Notre-Dame La Réal (Our Royal Lady), set the date for September 10, 1987, almost a year after my first retreat in Belloc. The wait had truly been worthwhile because the Holy Spirit granted me

[4] This area is not far from Toulouse in southern France. It is about fifteen kilometers from Castelnaudary.

the joy of seeing my entire family embrace the Catholic faith.

While we had been progressing toward the Catholic Church, our Baptist mission had been regressing. Jacques and Chafia were no longer coming regularly as a couple. Jacques sometimes came alone on Sundays, but his wife was being influenced by his mother, who had recently separated from her Baptist congregation and joined a Pentecostal church. I was preaching expositorily from the New Testament on matters in which I still believed, and I was not deviating from Baptist doctrine. This was not at all difficult, for I simply avoided those subjects, such as eschatology, over which Catholics and Baptists disagree. Nevertheless, my heart was somewhere else.

I received a letter from our church in Arkansas requesting information about a summer visit to the States they wanted us to make. Several supporting churches had written a few months earlier to ask if we were coming home, because they needed to work out a schedule for our visit. Now that so much had changed, I had to try to figure out the best way to go about terminating our relationship with these churches. How could I be honest with them and still provide for our family?

Before I could write to them, Monique and I left for a retreat the bishop asked us to make. He had suggested that, before we enter the Church, we make a retreat to prepare ourselves for the move. Over Pentecost, we stayed in a convent with a Catholic lay community founded by a former Protestant pastor and several others who had been Protestants. This community has an emphasis and style that come from both the Carmelite and charismatic spiritualities. They stress the Hebrew roots of the faith, the arts, evangelism, and a life of providence. At the time the community was called Lion of Judah. Since then it has been renamed the Beatitudes. Since its foundation, the Beatitudes has been enjoying tremendous growth (for France) and has foundations in several other countries. After two days with them, Monique and I went on to spend three days with the monks at Notre-Dame de Belloc.

On our way home, we had not gone more than thirty kilometers when we had an auto accident. A severe storm had struck the Basque region, and everywhere we looked there were downed trees. Monique was reading aloud the newspaper report about the storm, and my head was turned a little toward her. She looked up and saw that the traffic ahead had come to a stop. "Look out", she yelled. Overreacting, I slammed on the brakes, which caused us to skid on the wet pavement into the car in front of us. Fortunately, no one was hurt in the collision (we were not going fast at all), but the entire front end of our car was twisted to the side and bent inward. Our automobile would be out of commission for several months.

The necessity of waiting for the needed parts and getting the car repaired provided us a reason to delay a trip to the States. So I wrote to Central Baptist and explained that I could not give a firm date for the trip. This gave a little more time for everything to work out. I knew full well that there was no way they would understand our decision to become Catholic, so I wanted to let them know in the easiest way possible. Understanding their mentality and having seen already what happened when we left the Jehovah's Witnesses, I wanted to protect my family from any possible harassment. I knew full well we risked being vilified and maligned because of "going over to the enemy camp". And so I saw the need to avoid fruitless contacts, just to disappear.

In the end I decided to write a long, personal resignation letter to my pastor in Arkansas. I told him how much I loved the people at Central Baptist and how much I appreciated their love and generosity toward us. They had done more for us than any other church or group. They were not at fault for our decision, I explained. Study and prayer had brought about new convictions that we were conscience-bound to follow (Lk 9:23). I did not state directly that we were entering the Catholic Church. I just described the Church we were joining as the one Christ had founded, the one that everyone could see had a clear, indisputable history and the necessary organization to accomplish a worldwide mission work. If he concluded that the Catholic Church fit this description, then how could he blame us for joining it?

Summer had arrived, and it was time to abandon the mission office in town. Again we were the recipients of God's Providence and Christian charity. One evening, a couple of laypeople and a religious brother helped us carry out carton after carton of books and literature and a few pieces of furniture. Everything was taken to a farm where we had been offered some storage space. We didn't finish until 11 P.M. A week later we moved out of the apartment. A couple of priests, some religious brothers, and a few young people from the church moved our things to a parishioner's house. The house was up for sale and almost empty, and we were allowed to live there rent free for six months, just the time we needed to find a job and a place to live.

To prepare for our upcoming entrance into the Church, the children went to catechism classes. Monique, Jean-Philippe, and I went to confession. It had been thirty-five years since I had last received this sacrament. Jean-Philippe and Monique would enter the Church by receiving the sacraments of reconciliation and confirmation. They did not require baptism because Monique had been baptized in the Catholic Church as a baby and Jean-Philippe had been baptized by me in the name of the Father and the Son and the Holy Spirit. Daniel and Mireille, who had not yet been baptized, required this sacrament, and Monique and I were required to have our marriage vows validated by the Church.

This was difficult for Monique to accept. "What? You mean to tell me that I'm not married?" she protested.

On September 10, 1987, we entered the Church during a very memorable Mass at Notre-Dame La Réal that lasted two hours and forty minutes. Father Claude Jean-Marie and his community, which had charge of the parish, arranged everything. I read Paul VI's "*Credo* of the People of God" before the entire congregation. Daniel and Mireille received a new birth through baptism at the hands of our beloved bishop of Perpignan, Jean Chabbert. He then confirmed Monique and Jean-Philippe. Monique and I gave each other the sacrament of marriage. Seven priests concelebrated, including a Spanish Jesuit from Barcelona and my Benedictine friend, Father Marc. The monastic community in charge of the parish was also a charismatic community, which explains why there was a great emphasis on song. Afterward, everyone was invited into the courtyard for the French custom of celebrating with punch or something a little stronger. So Jesus, along with his mother Mary and all the saints, received my family into his visible Church. We were home, all of us!

The day after our entry into the Church, I began working in a Catholic high school. I was hired to help install a computer system designed to schedule classes for the school. I would also help out in the offices. I took this position at a time when the school administration was badly divided due to internal strife. It had been a long time since I had done secular work, and I couldn't help feeling somewhat unfaithful to my calling to France. After a time I adjusted to the job, and I enjoyed the computer work. I was hired on a ten-month limited contract, and when it expired I was out of a job. I had trained the secretaries to use various programs and the assistant director to oversee the scheduling program and now there was nothing more for me to do. In the budget squeeze I found myself unemployed.

When the house where we were staying finally sold, we looked for an apartment more in line with our new lifestyle. After a search that often left us discouraged, we found one that had everything we wanted. It was the cheapest apartment we had seen yet, *and* it was just across the street from Notre-Dame La Réal. I could arrive home in the evening just in time to attend daily Mass, which began at 6:15 P.M. After Mass we ate supper, spent time with the children, and concluded our day with family prayers. The chimney mantle served as our family altar. Over the mantle we had hung a crucifix and an icon of the Holy Family. Candles were placed along the mantle. This crucifix was a gift from my cousin, a Benedictine in New Hampshire, and the icon was given to us by the couple who are the godparents of our children. Every night we stood or knelt in front of our family altar for evening prayers. We sang the Our Father as we had learned to do in church and with the sisters. We had sold the television when we moved from Moulin-à-Vent, and we never replaced it. So we had lots of free time in the evenings to spend reading good books. We read stories by C. S. Lewis and J. R. R. Tolkien, lives of missionaries (Catholic and Protestant), and biographies of saints.

We were happy to participate in the parish activities led by Father Claude Jean-Marie's community. There was Tuesday night practice for singing the liturgy, a Wednesday morning catechism class for young children, and a Wednesday evening meeting for adolescents. Friday evenings were reserved for confessions. The parish held a vigil on Saturday evening in order to prepare Sunday's celebration. They sang the Psalms and certain hymns and prayers; this was a charismatic service in which there was opportunity for everyone to participate. The vigil could last from two to three hours and, coming at the end of the day, was sometimes quite physically tiring for me. The liturgy seemed to have been influenced by the Eastern Church: polyphonic singing, incense, and icons—which probably explains my continuing interest in the Eastern rites.

We started out attending everything, but we soon learned we had to pull back in order to spend time together as a family. Family time is precious and is worth safeguarding. It is a treasure easily lost or stolen. Little ones will not be with us forever, and parents have a sacred duty to train and educate them. We felt this to be our most important role. Yet we recognized that we were very fortunate to belong to such an active parish. Participating at Mass in such a parish strengthened us greatly. Our Masses were usually concelebrated by two or three priests, sometimes by as many as five. Two Sundays a month the parish scheduled a fellowship time in the courtyard of the church. There were Hebrew dances for the young and music and skits to entertain everyone. At about 3:30 P.M. they had a teaching, a film, or a play inside the church. I will always be grateful to this community for the great energy they unreservedly devoted to God's Kingdom. Their goal was to build a parish based on Acts 2, which speaks of the first disciples sharing everything.

As time went on, we felt drawn more and more to the community of the religious sisters who had also accompanied our family.[5] We loved them very much. We attended their liturgy as often as possible. Some people are drawn to one thing, and others to another. How happy we should all be that there are different spiritualities in the Catholic Church and that people can gravitate to one that appeals to them, the one that will help them to grow into strong and faithful Christians. Our family was drawn to the Community of the Lamb, which had about thirty lay associates. So, after praying about it, we applied for admission as lay members, and the bishop gave us his permission. During a summer camp, Monique and I made our promises and received a large

[5] Les Petites Soeurs de Saint Dominique, Communauté de l'Agneau, is the name in French.

*Two Sisters of St. Dominic talking with a homeless man
in the courtyard of Notre-Dame La Réal*

rosary and a little wooden cross to wear as a symbol of our belonging to this community. Sometimes the sisters' Divine Office lasted until midnight or even into the wee morning hours. We laypeople had the freedom to leave when we felt we needed to do so.

When my unemployment insurance began running out, and I saw that I didn't have much hope of finding work in that particular area, we considered returning to the United States or entering another community, which could support us in evangelism (our bishop had discussed this with us). The leaders of the Community of the Lamb thought that we should engage in some kind of ministry with them. It was not very clear how all this would work out, but we gratefully accepted this opportunity to serve God once again. We spent the next four years doing evangelism in our diocese.

Two other families in Perpignan were also members of our community. These people were a fine example to us from the very moment we entered the Church. We were able to observe how other families lived their Catholic faith. Our friends went to daily Mass, and their lives testified to their love of Jesus. Their sole desire was to follow the Lamb in poverty and humility. To fulfill more completely their commitment to put into practice their inspiration, they moved to a neighborhood where poverty and drugs abounded. This step was not only courageous but was proof that the Church had not abandoned the people there. Because we loved the members of our community and the Lord, we wanted to imitate their example as much as was practical for our family. We wanted to take our place with the poor and the needy, too, and to love them as did the Son of God, who, having left heaven's riches, became poor for our sakes in order that we might become rich, spiritually, in him. We met once a week in that neighborhood with these two couples for prayers, and often we got together on a Saturday evening to sing the *Lucernaire* (evening prayers at sunset). Perhaps they didn't always understand us North Americans and former Protestant fundamentalists. But it was good for all of us, and we needed the fellowship and the encouragement as much as anyone.

The lay members of the community contributed toward our support, and we spent time visiting in the poor neighborhood. As time passed, we responded to requests for visits from the outlying villages. This led us to establish weekly visits with former Jehovah's Witnesses, to offer them counsel and encouragement. They had so many questions. After we had spent four to six months with them, we tried to establish a systematic Bible study in their home. We usually took them through one of the books in the New Testament, using it to teach them how to study, all the while seeking to integrate them into a local parish. It was an eye-opener to see the brokenness and the suffering they had experienced. These people had a sincere desire to know the truth. Their attitudes and thought patterns revealed the extent to which they had been indoctrinated. Their association with the Jehovah's Witnesses had left them bitter and with very negative attitudes also toward the Catholic Church in which they had been raised.

Even though my phone number was unlisted, people who wanted to find me did. This led to a number of invitations to give conferences. I enjoyed challenging my audience in regard to our practice of Christianity, just as I had done as a pastor. I had the opportunity to travel and to visit other parishes throughout France.

These four years of ministry passed rapidly,[6] and then the Lord brought us into contact with another movement. One day we read an article about a new religious order, the "Legionaries of Christ". This is a congregation of priests that

---

[6] Jacques and Chafia and their children are now members of Notre-Dame La Réal parish. Father Marc is now meeting (1996) with a JW man as a result of a contact to whom I referred him. Our ministry in France continues through my writings there.

was founded in Mexico in 1941. We knew that our youngest son, Daniel, wanted to become a priest. He was an altar boy, and he showed a keen interest in spiritual things. This led us to contact the director of the Legionaries in France, Father Gouraud, who came to visit us during his travels in the south. Our conversation revealed that we enjoyed a certain harmony in ideas; so, after we studied the matter, we decided to send Daniel to their secondary school outside of Valencia, Spain. The school was called a "vocational school". In the past, it would have been called a minor seminary.

I told Daniel that, if he went to school in Valencia, I didn't want him to be crying to come home after three or four months. He was going for a year. If he liked it, he could stay; if he decided he wanted to come home, he could come home and pick up his education in France where he left off. We went down to see him as often as we could, and each time he surprised us by his progress in Spanish and in his desire to pursue his vocation with the Legionaries. It was not a whim but something that fulfilled what he really wanted to do. He was happy, surrounded by good comrades, and he had the spiritual direction he needed.

After about two years in Valencia, he reached his sixteenth birthday and was allowed to go on to Salamanca, where he entered the Legionaries' novitiate. The novitiate lasts two years. He put on the black cassock and became a real seminarian. As of this writing, Daniel is twenty years old, and he has completed the novitiate and two years of humanities in Salamanca, Spain. This year he is going to Rome to study philosophy, and he continues to be very happy with his decision to become a priest with the Legionaries of Christ. Even though the separation is hard for us as parents, especially because we are very close to our children, we consider it a privilege to offer what we love most to our heavenly Father. We pray that if this is his vocation, with God's grace he will become a worthy servant of God and his Church.

By this time, our eldest son, Jean-Philippe, was in school in Montpellier, where he was continuing his studies after high school. He was now on his own, pursuing his career. Mireille was the only child with us. So after consultation with Father Gouraud, we applied for an apostolate with the Legionaries. We were hoping to work in Spain, which would keep us close to our children. Their request to us was that we consider working in Mexico. We asked for time to pray about it, but after only twenty-four hours of prayer and discussion, we as a family accepted their proposal.

CHAPTER 15

Homeward Bound on El Camino Real:
Mexico and the United States

Leaving France was not easy. Our children had grown up there; we loved the people; and the country and its customs had become a part of our lives It would not be easy for our daughter. She had the most to give up, since France was all she had known since she was two years old. We had two months to prepare, get vaccinations, sell what we could, decide what we could take with us, reduce our belongings down to a reasonable size for shipping by boat, and get tickets; worst of all, we were leaving without a visa. This did put quite a strain on us, and it required a lot of faith. Besides, I wasn't very fluent in Spanish; I could read it fairly well, but I had not maintained any speaking ability since my studies about five years previously.

The Legionaries of Christ paid my trip to Rome so that I could get to know their community better, and they me at the same time. Also, it was planned that I would attend a conference on cults with some of their people. I did not make it to the conference, but I did enjoy the visit to the Vatican and, this time, finally visiting the bones of Saint Peter under the Basilica. Rome was now so much more meaningful to me than on the visit I had made when a Baptist. I was moved to tears as I worshipped and prayed at this most sacred shrine of Catholicism. The Legionaries took me around the city, and I saw many things that a tourist will see—the Coliseum, the catacombs, and the famous churches. I enjoyed very much seeing the Legionaries' Seminary in Rome, and now, as I think of my son going there to study, it is easy to see him at the Seminary in my imagination because I know the place.

We arrived in Mexico City during the fall in a dreary night's light rain. The director for the Legionaries' School of Faith was there, along with several people from the school where I was going to work for the next year. We were given two days in a fine hotel to rest and get acclimated somewhat while our apartment was being painted. The people in Mexico had not been sure of our arrival dates, and rentals in a suitable area were not easy to find. Only at the last minute had they found something for us.

Throughout the move there had been some difficulties in communications due to discussions being carried on in several countries. In the beginning it was not even sure we would be going to Mexico. I had been told to keep an open mind. But at last we arrived. The first thing I noted was the altitude. In fact, it would always be a problem for me because of the weakness I had in my legs. Although I no longer use a cane, my left leg has remained weak, and I have to exert more energy to do what someone else does easily. I found I was often out of breath, and my heart had to adjust. We would remain in Mexico for the next twenty months. We had an apartment on the fifth floor in a nice area of the city, not far from the zoo. Climbing five flights of stairs was no joke for me. Monique and Mireille adjusted far better than I. They had no problem taking a bus, but I did. It meant risking a bad fall, since the bus drivers didn't always come to a complete stop when letting passengers off. This was a constant fear I had to deal with. Finally I adjusted better to the altitude and the means of transportation and at the last began to get around a bit better. Still, all the while we were there, we never had a car or a telephone. We couldn't afford these, and we found the lack of them imposed a severe limitation on our lifestyle.

I was employed as an instructor in the catechetical school for the training of lay catechists. This meant that I often went outside of Mexico City to give classes in other cities. At times I took a plane to Tijuana, Ciudad de Obregón, Chihuahua, and Laredo, Mexico, an experience that gave me a good opportunity to meet the people across northern Mexico. Our classes included introduction to the Bible and history of the Church and the methodology of teaching. I also lectured on cults a number of times in some of the other catechetical schools. Several times I stayed for a few days or a week at a "hacienda" the school owned. I lived with the students whom we brought in from all over the country. They were usually from a poorer class but extremely devoted to the Catholic faith and desirous of learning and returning to teach their people. They were lodged and fed for six weeks while receiving their training. In Mexico City, I worked at the main offices for the school. I was in charge of investigation, but I had to struggle with it because I had not completely mastered the language; also, I preferred working on a different level with people. I didn't care much for theoretical sessions, where I felt disadvantaged linguistically.

Because of the cost of living (Mireille was in private school) and our lack of residency, the school released us to seek other employment and ministries more in line with our pastoral and missionary concerns. This brought us back to the States. I was actually seeking employment at the Eternal Word Television Network when I met Father Juan Rivas, L.C., through a contact. He asked me to work with him in evangelism through radio and conferences. God has certainly led us in surprising and unexpected ways.

We are now settled down in California but still struggling with the lack of universal medical insurance and salary limitations. We have come to appreciate better the difficulties and challenges many immigrants face when arriving in the States.

While still happily engaged in evangelism through conferences I continue to look to God, saying, "Lord, here am I. Send me" (Is 6). Where will his highway take us? We have journeyed from Europe, to Mexico, to California, following the King's Highway, *El Camino Real*. And, by God's grace, we intend to follow it forever in his holy Catholic Church.

Bibliography

Bibles

The Holy Bible, Authorized Version (*King James Version*). London: Oxford University Press. (Wide margins and center column containing marginal or alternate readings with references.)

The Holy Bible, Revised Standard Version (Catholic Edition). San Francisco: © 1965, 1966 Ignatius Press [1994].

The New American Bible (Saint Joseph Edition). New York: Catholic Book Publishing, 1987.

Reference Books

Abbott-Smith, G. *A Manual Greek Lexicon of the New Testament*. 3d ed. Edinburgh: T. & T. Clark, 1981.

Arndt, William, and William Gingrich, trans. *A Greek–English Lexicon of the New Testament and Other Early Christian Literature*. Bauer's 4th rev. and aug. ed. Chicago: University of Chicago, 1957.

Barnes, Albert. *Barnes' Notes on the New Testament*. Grand Rapids: Kregel Publications, 1975. Originally published in London.

Bickersteth, Edward Henry. *The Trinity*. Grand Rapids: Kregel Publications, 1957. Originally published as *The Rock of Ages, or Three Persons but One God*.

Dana, H. E., and Julius R. Mantey. *A Manual Grammar of the Greek New Testament*. New York: Macmillan, 1957.

Elwell, Walter A., ed. *Evangelical Dictionary of Theology*. Grand Rapids: Baker Book, 1984.

Englishman's Hebrew and Chaldee Concordance of the Old Testament. 5th ed. Grand Rapids: Zondervan, 1970.

Kittle, Gerhard, ed. *Theological Dictionary of the New Testament.* Translated and edited by Geoffrey W. Bromiley. Grand Rapids: Eerdmans, 1965.

Lenski, R. C. H. *The Interpretation of Acts of the Apostles.* Minneapolis, Minn.: Augsburg Publishing House, 1961.

Lightfoot, J. B., ed. and trans. *The Apostolic Fathers.* 5 vols. 1889–90. Reprints, Grand Rapids: Baker Book House, 1981.

Martin, Walter A. *The Kingdom of the Cults.* Rev. ed. Minneapolis: Bethany Fellowship, 1972.

Palmer, Edwin H. *The Five Points of Calvinism.* Enl. ed. Grand Rapids: Baker Book, 1980.

Robertson, A. T. *Word Pictures in the New Testament.* Nashville: Broadman Press, 1932.

Smith, J. B. *Greek–English Concordance to the New Testament: A Tabular and Statistical Greek–English Concordance Based on the King James Version with an English-to-Greek Index.* Scottdale, Pa.: Herald Press, 1977.

Thayer, Joseph Henry, ed. and trans. *A Greek–English Lexicon of the New Testament, Being Grimm's Wilke's Clavis Novi Testamenti.* 4th ed. 1901. Reprint, Grand Rapids: Zondervan, 1963.

Trench, Richard C. *Synonyms of the New Testament.* 9th ed. 1880. Reprint, Grand Rapids: Eerdmans, 1973.

Whiston, William, trans. *Josephus Complete Works.* Grand Rapids: Kregel Publications, 1974.

A SAMPLING OF CATHOLIC PUBLICATIONS

Christophe, Paul, S.J. *L'Église dans l'histoire des hommes.* 2 vols. Paris: Droguet-Ardant, 1982.

Jurgens, W. A. *The Faith of the Early Fathers.* 3 vols. Collegeville, Minn.: Liturgical Press, 1970.

Keating, Karl. *Catholicism and Fundamentalism: The Attack on "Romanism" by "Bible Christians".* San Francisco: Ignatius Press, 1984.

———. *What Catholics Really Believe: Setting the Record Straight.* San Francisco: Ignatius Press, 1995.

Morino, Msgr. Claudio. *Verbum Dei Semen.* 6 vols. Paris: Editions Téqui, 1986. (Very valuable for understanding Catholic teaching of the Scriptures and also for its many references to the Church Fathers.)

Nicolas, Jean-Hervé, O.P. *Synthèse dogmatique.* 2d ed. Fribourg and Paris: Editions Beauchesne, 1986.

Quasten, Johannes. *Patrology.* 2 vols. 1950. Reprint, Westminster, Md.: Christian Classics, 1983. Paperback ed., 1993.

Schreck, Alan. *Catholic and Christian: An Explanation of Commonly Misunderstood Catholic Beliefs.* Ann Arbor: Servant Books, 1984.

Sparks, Jack N., ed. *The Apostolic Fathers.* 1978. Reprint, Minneapolis: Light and Life Publishing, n.d.

Wiseman, Cardinal Nicholas. *Lectures on the Principal Doctrines and Practices of the Catholic Church.* Two vols. in one. 6th American ed., Baltimore, 1870.

Wuerl, Donald W. *Fathers of the Church.* Boston: Daughters of St. Paul, 1982. (Very simple introduction.)

This Rock (magazine). Catholic Answers, P.O. Box 17490, San Diego, CA, 92111. (This is an excellent source for Catholic apologetics.)

INTERNET ADDRESSES AND WEB PAGES

Catholic Answers of San Diego, Calif., can be found at:

http://www.electriciti.com/~answers

James Akin, who works with Catholic Answers, has a home page at:

http://www.io-online.com/james/index.htm

Information on JWs (Protestant sources) is located at:

> http://www.nano.no/~telemark/DnSEng.html
> http://www.cam.org/~pinnacl/beyondjw.htm
> http://www.ultranet.com/~comments
> http://ourworld.compuserve.com/homepages/
>   chris_arndt/

To search the Scriptures in different versions on the Internet try:

> http://www.gospelcom.net/bible

For Church Fathers:

> http://www.iclnet.org/pub/resources/christian-
>   history.html

For Catholic Encyclopedia (1913):

> http://www.knight.org/advent/cathen/cathen.htm

For Catholic files, Church Fathers, and Vatican News:

> http://ewtn.com